STEPHEN HENDRY

SNOOKER MASTERCLASS

Stephen Hendry

Snooker Masterclass

BLOOMSBURY

First published in Great Britain 1995
Bloomsbury Publishing Plc,
2 Soho Square,
London W1V 6HB

A CIP catalogue record for this book is available from the British Library

ISBN 0 7475 1870 X

Designed by Bradbury and Williams
Designer: Bob Burroughs

Printed in Great Britain by
Butler & Tanner Ltd, Frome

Contents

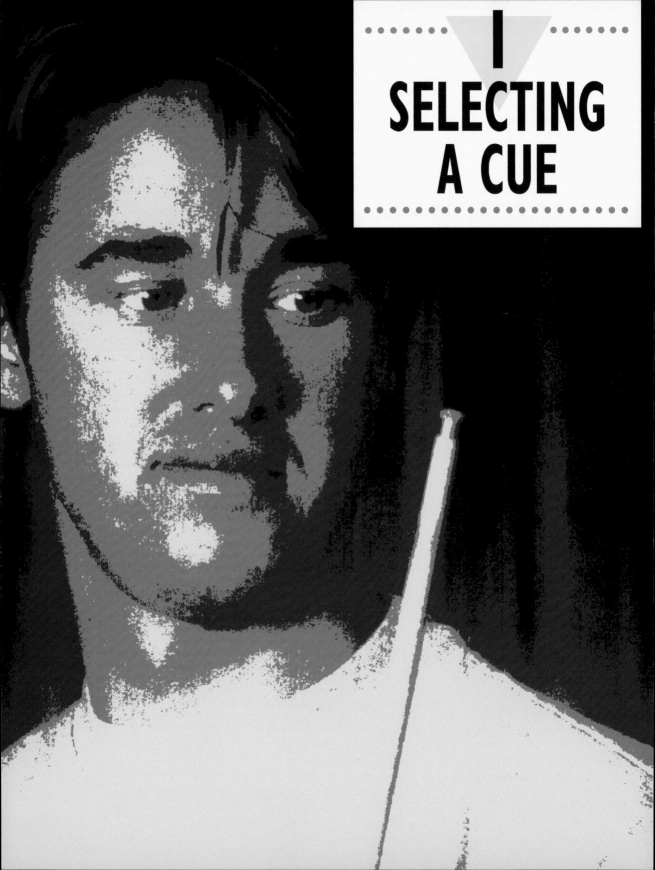

I
SELECTING
A CUE

Every year you hear stories of famous sportsmen and women signing lucrative contracts with sports goods manufacturers to endorse and use their products. Nick Faldo won the US Masters and British Open golf championships using Wilson clubs, yet abandoned them less than twelve months later, after signing a multi-million dollar deal with Mizuno.

It is very unusual for a top snooker professional to swap and change a cue with which he has been successful. When I had my cue stolen from a hotel in Reading during the 1990 Rothmans Grand Prix, people say that my face was ashen. That told its own story.

My manager, Ian Doyle, immediately offered a £10,000 reward for information leading to its return, and when I was eventu-

'It is vitally important to select a cue with which you feel comfortable and then stick with it.'

ally re-united with my cue at a press conference two days later, my relief was immense. I grabbed the cue, kissed it and said that I'd never leave my baby again. A bit dramatic? This was how I felt. A couple of weeks later there really was a happy ending when I beat Nigel Bond 10-5 to win the title.

Other players in the top bracket, such as Alex Higgins, Ray Reardon and John Spencer, have suffered a dramatic decline in fortunes after having their cues damaged or stolen.

This strong bond between a particular player and his cue also exists amongst amateurs, so when taking up the game, it is vitally important quickly to select a cue with which you feel comfortable and then stick with it. Look after it well, use no other and, assuming your original

choice is correct, your game and general performance will benefit.

Selecting the ideal cue is a matter of personal choice. Players with only a minimal interest in the game and who do not play often are quite content to knock the balls around with one of the communal cues to be found in most snooker clubs. But a player with any ambition at all must make the investment of purchasing his own cue; this is his only hope of increasing consistency and

Me and my cue – it might not be the most expensive in the world but to me it's invaluable.

improving his standard. Each cue has its own peculiarities, so by using a different one each time you play, it is impossible to gauge reactions and gain confidence.

My advice is to choose one which reaches between two and three inches above shoulder level. It should weigh between sixteen and nineteen ounces, although in the modern game, where power plays a big part, sixteen ounces might just be on the light side. Remember, though, that these are merely guidelines, not hard and fast rules.

The optimum weight and length of a cue are different for different players. Mr X may think a particular cue is perfectly balanced, while Mr Y feels it is a broomstick. Joe Davis, world champion from 1927 to 1946, maintained that a cue with an abnormally thick butt should be avoided, as should one which tapers down, forming a very small tip to be used. I agree with him. The thick-butted cue often makes for an uncomfortable grip, while a thin tip compromises a player's ability to pull off power shots.

The best cues are made from ash or maple. Until the 1970s, the one-piece cue was used by virtually every player. However, with the strides in cue technology and the demand for a more easily transportable cue, two-piece cues, with either a stainless steel or wooden joint, are now very common. My cue is a one-piece, but Steve Davis, Jimmy White and John Parrott all use two-piece cues – and they can't all be wrong. The final point when selecting an ash cue: make sure the grain of the wood is running from butt to tip, otherwise you could have problems.

It is wise, when purchasing your cue, to try it out before a decision is made, and it is sometimes better to buy a cue from a snooker club which stocks a wide variety for sale to the general public. With the tables there to practise on, it is easier to experiment and discover the cue with which you feel most at ease.

Once you have purchased a cue, don't feel that you are duty bound to persevere with it if you begin to think the original choice was incorrect. It is true that sticking with one cue promotes consistency, while indiscriminate swapping is no long-term solution. However, when a cue is patently not suitable, don't be afraid to seek out a replacement. One thing is for sure: if you do find the ideal cue, it pays to look after it well.

Keeping the cue as it should be is simple enough and not that time-consuming. All that is needed is an occasional wipe with a damp cloth, to stop the cue becoming sticky, and an on-going shaping of the cue-tip.

Keep the cue safe from theft or damage – I've certainly learned my lesson – and always bear in mind that extreme temperatures can cause the cue to warp. Many a player has found this out the hard way after leaving his cue in the car overnight. Damage, loss and theft of your cue will cause havoc in your game. Having to go through the re-adjustment to another cue is, 99 per cent of the time, a frustrating, confidence-sapping experience, during which it's inevitable that form suffers badly.

> DON'T BE PUT OFF BY PRICE. IF A CUE IS AT THE CHEAPER END OF THE PRICE SCALE, IT DOESN'T NECESSARILY MEAN THAT IT IS POOR AND NOT THE ONE FOR YOU. LOOK AT MINE FOR INSTANCE. REMEMBER THAT ONE MAN'S WINE IS ANOTHER'S POISON WHEN IT COMES TO THE SELECTION OF CUES.

'One thing is for sure: if you do find the ideal cue, it pays to look after it well.'

CHECK LIST

THE CUE

1. A useful guideline is that the cue should reach two or three inches above shoulder level and be between sixteen and nineteen ounces in weight.

2. Avoid thick butts and narrowly tapered cues which force small tips.

3. Don't be frightened to change your cue if you are not happy with it. Mix perseverance with common sense.

4. Always look after your cue. Warping, damage or theft of your cue can have a disastrous effect on your game.

THE TIP

A player can have the best, most finely balanced cue imaginable, but if it has a defective tip it is useless.

In modern times, the best tips have traditionally been manufactured with the names Blue Diamond and Elkmaster. Professionals prefer a hard tip to a soft, spongy one, which compromises the

IN ORDER TO STOP YOURSELF MISCUEING, CHALK MUST BE APPLIED TO THE TIP OF YOUR CUE EVERY TWO OR THREE SHOTS. THIS ALLOWS THE TIP TO GRIP THE CUE-BALL. NEXT TIME YOU WATCH ME ON TELEVISION, YOU MAY NOTICE THAT I CHALK THE CUE ALMOST SUBCONSCIOUSLY. IT IS SOMETHING WE HAVE DONE THOUSANDS OF TIMES BEFORE.

THE USA PRODUCES THE BEST CHALK AVAILABLE IN BRAND NAMES KNOWN AS TRIANGLE OR NATIONAL TOURNAMENT. CHALK COMES IN A VARIETY OF COLOURS BUT, WITHOUT DOUBT, GREEN IS BEST. BLUE CHALK TENDS TO STICK TO THE CUE-BALL, INCREASING THE LIKELIHOOD OF KICKS — BAD CONTACTS BETWEEN WHITE AND OBJECT-BALL. GIMMICKY RED AND BEIGE CHALKS ARE ALSO ON THE MARKET, BUT AS THESE LEAVE MARKS ON THE CLOTH WHICH ARE EXTREMELY TOUGH TO BRUSH OUT, I CAN'T RECOMMEND THEM.

ability to apply sidespin and backspin, or accurately gauge shot strength. While harder tips are definitely preferable, beware of excessively hard tips which cause the cue-ball to skid.

When you buy a cue, it is very rare to find the tip exactly to your satisfaction. You must gently dome it, maybe with a piece of sandpaper. This important operation takes around five or ten minutes and it's well worth the time.

Always keep an eye on your tip and make sure that it is nicely domed and not chipped or damaged in any way.

RESTS AND EXTENSIONS

Unlike those of pool tables, the dimensions of snooker tables are such that artificial implements are sometimes needed to enable a player to play successfully an awkwardly placed shot. Without help, some shots would be impossible.

The normal rest, an accessory which each table possesses, measures around five feet and has an X-shaped head of plastic or, more commonly, steel. These rest-heads act as replacements for the bridge hand, their purpose being to hold the cue firmly in place. I passionately dislike plastic rests, as their lack of weight limits stability.

Being able to use the rest well is essential for any player bidding to attain a high standard. Confidence is a massive factor with the rest and to this end Nigel Gilbert is an innovator. Gilbert, a professional from Bedford with a solid all-round game, is one of that rare group

Applying the extension to my cue is easy enough.

Most extensions these days are designed to fit snugly around all sizes of cues.

number of intervening balls (i.e. the pack of reds).

The half-butt and threequarter-butt are brought into action when, because the cue-ball is a long way out of reach, the ordinary rest is not long enough. These are the most cumbersome implements – I hate using them – not only because of their length (sometimes up to ten feet), but also because the mis-shapen tip and instability of the rest makes anything other than the simplest of shots almost impossible, even for the

> **'Being able to use the rest well is essential for any player bidding to attain a high standard.'**

most talented players. In the light of this, the comparatively recent development of the cue extension has been a godsend, making the half and threequarter-butt virtually redundant.

Professionals, and indeed most seriously minded amateurs, own an extension which fits snugly on to the butt of their cue. We have a significant advantage over those players who do not have extensions. The advantage is that, as never previously, the player's own cue-tip, with its greater responsiveness compared to that of the 'long rests', can be used for nearly every shot, regardless of awkwardness.

who carry a personal rest from tournament to tournament. It has a marginally smaller head than normal and he clearly feels at home using it. Gilbert, though, is an exception. Usually a rest comes with the table, not the player.

Apart from the regular rests, others – known as the spider, the half-butt and threequarter-butt – are also available, but they are employed less frequently.

The spider, of which there are a number of different types, affords the player an opportunity to cue over an intervening ball by providing an artificially high bridge. The swan-neck spider gives the highest of all bridges while the extended spider, sometimes called the branding iron, allows a player to bridge over a

CHECK LIST

TIP, CHALK AND EXTENSION

1. The best cue is no use without a good tip.

2. Dome your tip and do not neglect it.

3. Always use green chalk, never red or beige.

4. Buying an extension is an invaluable investment.

2

THE STANCE, BRIDGE AND GRIP

illions of people in many countries are now snooker-playing regulars, yet only a very small percentage are able to play to the kind of high standard where a century break is within their capabilities. For most of the game's under-achievers, the reason lies in a lack of practice, the misapplication of basic principles, or a combination of both.

As with bad cueing habits, an awkward stance or a weak bridge is difficult to rectify, and it does not take a genius to work out the paramount importance of concentrating on getting the basics right from the very start.

A player of, say, five years' experience may try hard to eradicate technical faults

but, subconsciously and especially under pressure, there is always the tendency to revert to bad habits. There are no inflexible rules governing bridge, stance and grip, but a player must work within a framework of orthodoxy to determine what is best and most effective for him.

THE STANCE

Unless you stand in the correct manner and also deliver the cue through the ball correctly, you will find it difficult to progress, regardless of how many practice hours you put in.

Of the professionals I've seen, which is most, I would have to say Australia's John Campbell, who is 6ft 4in tall, has easily the widest stance. Mine is much

---

THE STANCE

● Varying heights of players obviously mean that the ideal stance is not the same for all, although the basic principles apply. Balance, flexibility and stability are all promoted and developed by a solid stance. The same basics apply to snooker as they do in shooting or boxing.

First, place your feet comfortably but not too far apart. The body weight should be as evenly distributed as possible and the body itself nicely balanced, in order that the only movement during the stroke will be made by the cue arm. When you bend forward and get your chin well down over the cue, your front leg (the left for a right-hander) should be slightly bent while the rear leg should be

Above: From this side view of my stance, you will notice that my back leg is pretty stiff, with my bent front leg taking most of the weight.

straighter. This back leg gives the maximum stability to a stance. Its foot should be turned out slightly but in the ordinary stance position kept firmly to the floor.

The front foot should be pointing in the general direction of the shot and

always be careful to keep your chest as side-on to the shot as you can. If your cue runs under the middle of your chin, your weight, like mine, should be more on your left (front) leg than your right. Steve Davis maintains that, in his snooker stance position, it would be virtually impossible for

someone to push him over from the front because of his stability and balance. These qualities are imperative for a good stance, as is the relative position of your feet. The two most common stance faults – apart from bending both knees cowboy style – are to have the feet too near or too far apart.

Below: From this side view of my stance, you can see how stable it is. This is vital if a stance is going to work for you.

Back view of the stance. The ideal stance should be one where your feet are not too far apart or too close together. As you can see from these exaggerated stances, a player finds it difficult if his feet are wide open or if his stance is too narrow.

narrower, but neither of us is wrong. Within the rough guidelines of orthodoxy, we have each discovered the most effective stance for ourselves.

When you take up any sport for the first time, snooker included, it is easy to fall into the trap of trying to copy your favourite player. In writing this book, it is not my intention to produce an army of Stephen Hendry clones.

Remember, physical attributes play a major part in the stance you adopt, so what might work for one player fails for another. Never be afraid to ask the opinion of a better player, experiment if needs be and with time you will develop the style that suits you best.

Bear this in mind, though: all effective stances should allow your cue to run through the ball as horizontally as possible. Get the cue brushing lightly against your chest. This is an aid to straight cueing and is absolutely essential if you are going to play the game well. Not everyone can become world champion or a well-paid professional, but it is my expe-

rience, from meeting many club players in exhibitions around the country, that the better one plays, the more enjoyment – and definitely the more satisfaction – you get from snooker.

THE BRIDGE

While idiosyncrasies exist with the grips and stances of different players, the bridge is usually the same. The role of the bridge is twofold. It helps you deliver the cue and, acting as the front part of a tripod – the other two parts being the player's legs – it gives a stance greater stability.

THE GRIP

The last, but most certainly not least important, of the three basics is the grip. There are different grips, and I'm often asked such questions as, 'Where do I hold the cue?' or 'How tightly do I need to grip it?'

Personally, I hold the cue around an inch from the butt for long shots and around three inches from the butt when

THE BRIDGE — MY ADVICE

● Making a workable bridge is straightforward enough. Place your hand flat on the table and spread your fingers as wide as possible without becoming uncomfortable. Keeping the fingers nicely spread, raise your knuckles above the surface of the table and cock the thumb high to form a channel between thumb and forefinger. This provides a groove for the cue to run through when a shot is played. Your bridge hand should be resting on the fingertips, the heel of the hand and the underpart of the thumb.

● By gripping the cloth reasonably firmly with the fingertips and by keeping the bridge arm straight, the bridge will be stable. I and many other modern professionals have a relaxed bridge. We do not consciously dig into the cloth like some of the older players. Fred Davis, winner of the World Championship eight times between 1948 and 1956, was noted for leaving marks on the cloth, so fierce was his grip.

● When you form the channel between thumb and forefinger, it is important to make sure that it is not too wide. If it is, the cue will wobble and the straightness of your cueing will be affected. Likewise, do not raise the bridge hand so high that it forces you to strike down on to the cue-ball causing unwanted spin to be imparted. The net result of all this is inaccuracy and frustration.

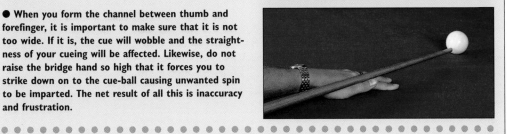

For long shots I hold the cue close to the butt.

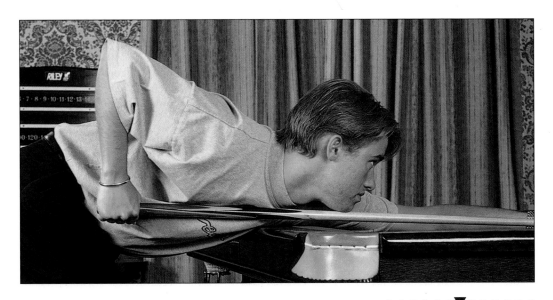

When I'm in around the reds, though, I tend to shorten up a bit and hold the cue two inches further from the butt.

I'm in close, because that gives me more 'feel' – and not too tightly. If you grip the cue too strongly you are undoubtedly susceptible to 'snatching' in pressure situations. I believe a looser, fluid grip like mine enables a player to cue with rhythm, tempo and above all else consistency.

On the other hand, it does not pay to hold the cue too lightly. With the modern game requiring a player to complete a whole range of power shots, such as deep screws and stuns, some strength in the grip is needed. I'm sure that James Wattana would be the first to admit that if he does have a weakness it is a comparative lack of cue-power. He also has a relaxed grip. The compromise between power and flexibility is ultimately one

you will, by trial and error, have to fathom out for yourself.

Whether the cue is held towards the palm or towards the fingertips often depends on a player's physical make-up rather than personal choice. If your wrist

'A looser, fluid grip like mine enables a player to cue with rhythm, tempo and above all else consistency.'

tends to turn inwards, like that of six-times world champion Ray Reardon and the 1993 Asian Open champion Dave Harold, you will prefer to grip the cue closer to the palm. If, however, you are like me and your wrist naturally turns outwards it is the fingertips that will be

If you've just taken up the game and you are still unsure about the best grip, just pick up your cue upright holding it about an inch from the butt and develop your grip from that.

brought into play. What may seem ungainly for one player may be perfectly comfortable for another.

One universal problem encountered by all players at some time or other is that of clutching the cue too tightly on power shots. When you do that, timing,

straightness of cue-action and general accuracy fly out of the window, causing this shot to go badly astray.

Today, to a lesser or greater extent, all of the world's leading professionals adopt a grip method which enables them to pull off these spectacular shots. To retain

fluency and reduce tension in the cue-arm the grip of one, two or sometimes three fingers is relaxed from the cue during the backswing and is reapplied as the cue is being propelled towards the cue-ball.

Novices need not be unduly concerned about these advanced shots, but even they can benefit by realising the importance of finding the right balance between the fierce and loose extremes of grip. As with most things on the technical side of snooker, a player needs to search for a suitable compromise.

The biggest fault amongst beginners is that they grip the cue too tightly.

A loose, but still support-ive, grip like mine helps a player to keep his cue-action rhythmical, not jerky as with a fierce grip.

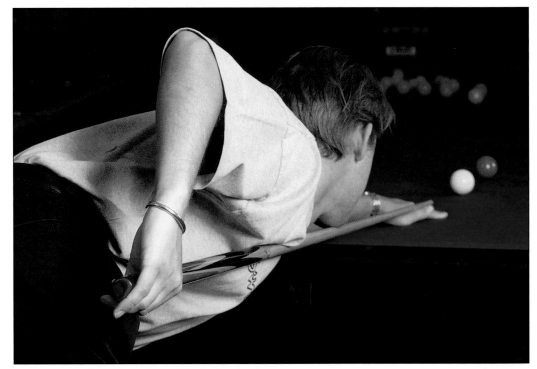

From the back, you can see that I relax my grip on the back-swing to reduce tension before I re-apply a stronger grip as the cue is being pushed through to make the stroke.

CHECK LIST

STANCE

1. Your feet should not be too close together or, indeed, too far apart.

2. Your weight should be distributed so that the only movement during the shot is made by the cue-arm.

3. A bent front leg and a straighter back leg help ensure greater stability.

4. Do not try to copy your favourite player, but develop the stance that is best suited for you.

BRIDGE

1. Spread your fingers as wide as possible without making it uncomfortable.

2. Raise the knuckles above the surface of the table and cock thumb high to form a channel for the cue to run through.

3. Grip the cloth firmly but not too fiercely.

4. Do not make the channel between thumb and forefinger too wide, or the cue will wobble when you play your shot.

5. Do not raise bridge hand so high that it forces you to strike down on the cue-ball.

GRIP

1. Hold the cue a couple of inches from the butt and not too tightly.

2. It is important to keep your wrist flexible but firm.

3. Do not clutch the cue too tightly for power shots.

4. To reduce tension and increase your fluency, release the grip of one, two or even three fingers on the backswing before reapplying their grip as you propel the cue towards the cue-ball.

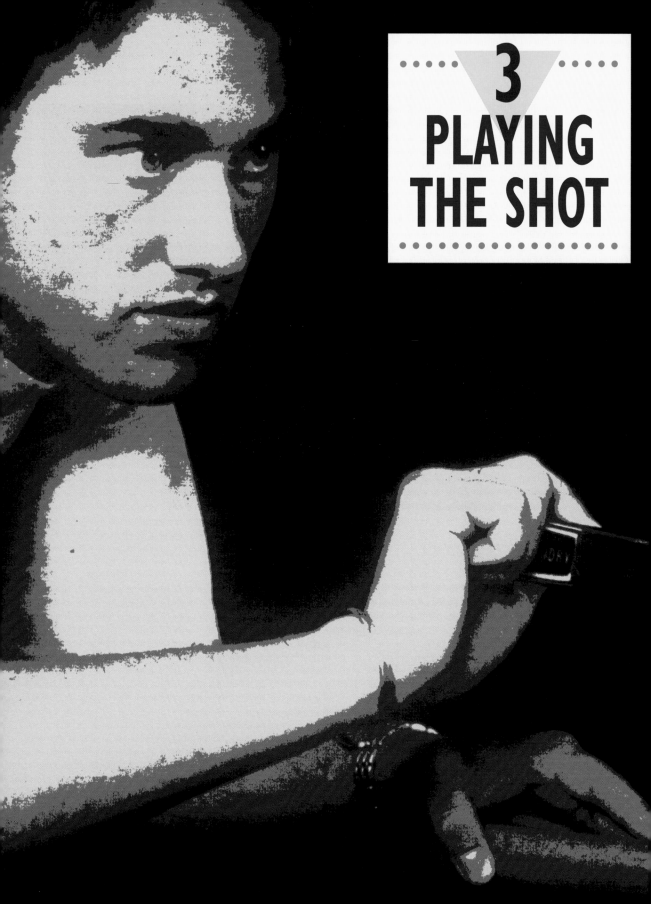

3
PLAYING
THE SHOT

Learning to pot is the thing that all raw novices, quite naturally, want to do as quickly as possible, for all players, whatever their standard, enjoy the sight and sound of pots going into pockets. It is without doubt the most satisfying and important aspect of snooker.

The ability to play a tight safety game and be a competent positional player is crucial, but if you cannot pot you will never be successful. I always think that having safety and positional capabilities without a keen potting eye is like having a million pounds without having anything spend it on.

Before you learn to sight the shot and develop a workable cue-action, just spend some time rechecking the basics - grip, bridge and stance. Remember your stance should be comfortable and stable, with your bridge between six and eight inches from the cue-ball. Finger pads should be gripping the cloth, with knuckles raised and thumb cocked to form a channel between it and the forefinger. Finally, always beware of a grip which is either too loose or too fierce. When these are sorted out, it's time to embark on the next phase of snooker's learning process.

MY TIP ON SIGHTING

Over the years it has become the norm for beginners to cue under the middle of the chin and nose so that both eyes can concentrate equally on the shot in hand. However, this makes the assumption –

SIGHTING

● Having the perfect cue-action but the worst alignment is useless. The bottom line is that you have got to know where to aim to pot. It could not be simpler.

On my travels I've seen a number of players with stylish, orthodox cue-actions who, because their aim is consistently wrong, regularly miss the target. Failure to pot well leads these players to think the fault lies with their technique, and even though this is not the case, they tinker, make certain alterations and the problems magnify. It is logical that, even with the straightest cue delivery possible, a player will struggle if he is the victim of defective sighting.

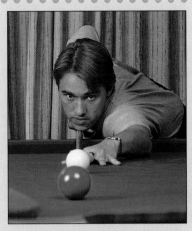

I am even-sighted which means that my cue runs directly beneath my chin. However, some players favour either their right or left eye - the master eye, and therefore cue beneath it.

wrongly in many cases – that the player enjoys equal strength in both eyes, while in fact many people have one, a master eye, which is considerably stronger than the other. I fall into the even-sighted category, like the majority of my professional colleagues. But Joe Davis and Rex Williams, a former world billiards champion, were pronounced left-eyed sighters, while John Virgo and Steve Newbury are among those who cue under their right eye.

It is simple to find out which is your master eye. Place a piece of chalk on the top cushion, go and stand in front of it at the baulk end of the table and point a finger at the block of chalk while making sure both eyes are kept open. When

'Having safety and positional capabilities without a keen potting eye is like having a million pounds but nothing to spend it on.'

you are focused on the chalk, close your left eye. If your finger remains pointing at the chalk you are right-eyed. To make doubly sure of this, just open your left eye and close your right. You will find that you have to move your finger to get it back on line with the chalk.

By discovering which, if any, is your master eye, you will be able to eradicate any sighting defects. If you are not sighting directly over the cue any player, even one with an effective cue-action, has a strong tendency to impart unwanted sidespin to the cue-ball by striking diagonally across it.

If your alignment and sighting of the shot are absolutely spot on, you will benefit from a straight cue-action. Before striking the cue-ball, line up the cue and make a number of preliminary addresses. These help your cueing become smooth and rhythmical, enhance the concentration and, most crucial of all, promote steadiness.

When you are actually playing the shot, you must switch your eyes from the cue-ball to the object-ball and back again. Always remember that only your eyes and not your head should move. I believe that at the last instant you should be looking at the spot on the object-ball where contact with the cue-ball needs to be made in order for the pot to be successful.

In golf the opposite is true. If while putting a player looks at the hole – his intended target and the equivalent of the

object-ball – he is most likely to miss. Whatever instructional book you choose to read, the author – myself included – will try to impress on you the value of limiting head movement to a minimum.

Many a television director has highlighted a particular idiosyncrasy of mine which involves flicking my eyes back and forth between pocket and object-ball before a shot. I do that when I'm down on the shot, as I always have, but when the shot is actually played my eyes are firmly fixed on the object-ball. That is a must.

CLIFF THORBURN, WHO HANDED ME ONE OF THE HEAVIEST DEFEATS OF MY CAREER, 9-1 IN THE SEMI-FINALS OF THE 1987 BCE INTERNATIONAL, CAN TELL YOU A HORROR STORY ABOUT APPLYING UNINTENTIONAL SIDESPIN ON EVERY SHOT.
CLIFF, WHO BECAME THE FIRST OVERSEAS PLAYER TO CAPTURE THE WORLD TITLE WHEN HE WON AT THE CRUCIBLE IN 1980, FELL TO 80TH IN THE PROVISIONAL RANKINGS BEFORE A COACH POINTED THIS TECHNICAL DEFICIENCY OUT TO HIM. ONCE CLIFF STOPPED STRIKING THE CUE-BALL UNINTENTIONALLY LEFT OF CENTRE, HE BEGAN TO CLIMB BACK UP THE RANKINGS AGAIN.

These three photographs, taken from behind, clearly show the importance of remaining still on the shot, and not moving your upper body, during the back swing, impact with the cue-ball and follow through.

THE CUE SWING

● The actual movement of
the cue, on the shot itself, is
best described as being like
the motion of a hinge opening
and closing. Basically the
shoulder, and indeed all of
the upper body and head,
should be kept as still as
possible while the cue-arm
acts as a pendulum swinging
to and fro.

Depending, of course, on
the type of shot required, the
cue-action should be as com-
pact as possible. The wrist of
your grip hand should be
flexible enough to allow the
cue to run parallel with the
surface of the table.

The hinge analogy works if
you visualise your elbow as
the hinge opening and closing
as the shot is carried out. The
hinge opens on the back-
swing, it is closing as the cue
strikes the white, and it is
fully closed at the completion
of the follow through.

CUE-ACTION

If you can rely on accurate sighting and your cue-action is both straight and true, you are well on the way to becoming an accomplished player.

As I've already pointed out, it is important, in order to aid sighting and foster steadiness on the shot, to make a number of preliminary addresses at the ball before each stroke is actually played.

Tony Knowles uses a large number of these 'feathering' movements, while John Parrott and Jimmy White make only a few. Speaking from personal preference, I find that too many addresses are counter-productive. Instead of serving to harness concentration and help alignment, they create indecisiveness, particularly on an important shot.

In golf, a game I also love, all good coaches emphasise the importance of letting the club do the work. The same principle applies in snooker, in which the cue should be propelled through the shot by the movement of the cue-arm, predominantly from wrist to elbow –

not the rest of the body. Any movement of the head or upper body is disastrous.

Many amateur players, whose enthusiasm for the game outweighs their ability to play it, will be so keen to see the result of a particular shot that they will raise their head before the shot has been completed.

It would be foolish to suggest that good players don't lift their heads occasionally, but this is rare at top level. It usually happens on a shot on which a player is feeling exceptional anxiety.

'No one is perfect, but the secret is to limit your technical problems to a minimum.'

Unwanted upper body movement is not the only problem that can beset a player's cue action; faults can also be found in the actual delivery of the cue, mainly in the backswing. Remembering that a smooth, rhythmical action is to be

THE EXTRAORDINARY STEPS TAKEN BY STEVE DAVIS TO CUT HEAD MOVEMENTS AT AN EARLY STAGE OF HIS PLAYING DEVELOPMENT ARE WELL-KNOWN ON THE CIRCUIT. DAVIS, ARGUABLY THE MOST TECHNICALLY AWARE PLAYER IN THE GAME, WOULD PLAY SHOT AFTER SHOT WHILE HIS PATIENT FATHER, BILL, HELD A CUE A FEW CENTIMETRES ABOVE HIS HEAD.

IF, EVEN ON A FORCING SHOT, STEVE'S HEAD CAME INTO CONTACT WITH THE HOVERING CUE, HE WOULD KNOW THERE HAD BEEN SOME HEAD MOVEMENT. WITH REMARKABLE SINGLE-MINDEDNESS AND SELF-DISCIPLINE HE WOULD CONTINUE TO PLAY THESE SHOTS UNTIL THE FLAW WAS IRONED OUT.

aimed for, it is obvious that jerky movements of the cue as it is drawn back are bound to cause problems. If you do not bring the cue back straight, what chance do you have of bringing it through straight?

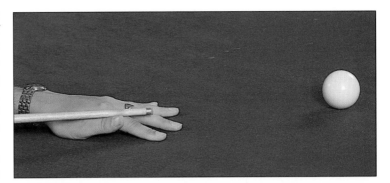

The cue should be taken back fluently, but not well past the horizontal. Then, after a fraction of a second's pause, commence its forward momentum towards the white. Keeping on the same line, the cue should go through the white – never jab at it – and come to rest after several inches. The whole process is simple enough. The key words are rhythm, fluency and above all, straightness.

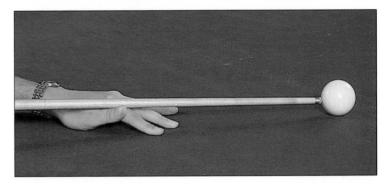

In his book *Tackle Snooker*, former world champion John Pulman advises his readers to practise their cue-actions, with imaginary balls, for anything up to three weeks before they play. I can't help feeling that this is not much use, because without testing anything in a real situation it is impossible to know whether it is working. Play as much as you can from day one, for it is only by playing that your game will improve.

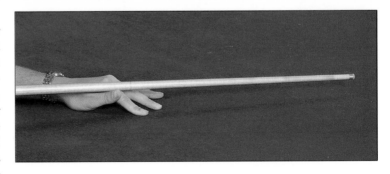

I took up snooker at the age of thirteen and looking back on it, while I obviously had some natural aptitude, in common that of with every other novice, my cue-action was extremely suspect. With constant practice it improved and gradually all my elementary technical errors disappeared. This is not to say I don't have any faults in my cue-action now. No one is perfect, but the secret in snooker, as it is in all sports, is to limit your technical problems to a minimum. If you feel strongly that a minor adjustment could pay off, then try it out. There's always room for improvement, even in the cue-actions of leading professionals.

4
THE
THEORY OF
POTTING

Regardless of your ability to play safe or manoeuvre the cue-ball into good positions, you will never make a top-class player if you cannot pot well. Potting allows big breaks to be compiled and, although positional play is of obvious importance, a beginner is best advised to concentrate his initial attention on potting.

The point on the object-ball that has to be struck for an attempted pot to be successful is that which is furthest away from the pocket. Theorists say that, to discover this point, you should trace an imaginary line from the centre of the pocket through the middle of the object-ball. Where this comes out is where the cue-ball should be aimed.

You don't have to know much about geometry to work out the most simple pot – at least in terms of computing the angle of contact required. With the dead straight pot, cue-arm, cue, cue-ball, object-ball and pocket should be in a straight line. A full-ball contact, i.e. one where the cue-ball covers the whole of the object-ball at the moment of impact, is needed. However, dead straight pots represent only a small percentage of those you will have to play.

On occasions three-quarter, half or quarter-ball contacts are required. Assuming a threequarter ball contact is needed, the cue-ball must be covering threequarters of the object-ball on impact. If the white strikes the object-ball so that it covers something more than threequarters, it is said to have been struck too full and the attempted pot will be undercut. On the other hand, if the cue-ball covers less than threequarters, too 'thin' a contact is

A dead straight pot. Notice that in this shot my cue-arm, cue, cue-ball, object-ball and pocket are in a straight line.

> *'Although positional play is of obvious importance, a beginner is best advised to concentrate his initial attention on potting.'*

A just off-straight pot.

made and the ball is said to have been overcut. If this is the case, the object-ball will miss the pocket on the opposite side to that if it had been undercut.

For potting there is absolutely no substitute for actual playing experience. As the novice goes through a period of trial and error in the early stages, there will no doubt be many times where misjudgement rather than poor cueing will cause a pot to be missed.

Novices encounter a lot of problems with the thin snick and quite often miss the red completely. After a while, judging these shots becomes much easier.

With this kind of half-ball pot, the cue-ball must cover half of the object ball on contact for the shot to be pulled off successfully.

All players have to learn the hard way about potting angles, and the important thing for the newcomer is to avoid frustration. After a while, pots that posed a problem at the start begin to look easy; angles which once baffled become clear.

The crucial thing is to benefit from your mistakes. Instead of becoming irate when a supposedly simple pot is missed, note what went wrong and make the necessary adjustments the next time you are faced with a similar shot. I must admit that when I began to play, I found my frequent misses extremely galling,

but I stuck with it and started getting more confident. Only with a reserve of experience and practice can you hope to begin to unravel the subtleties of the art of potting.

PRACTISE YOUR CUE-ACTION AND POTTING

Test your cue-action

How can you tell if your cue-action, the most vital cog in the machinery of potting balls, has developed a fault?

The first practice exercise could not be more simple or, indeed, illuminating. A player has to place the cue-ball on the brown spot. He then strikes it at a moderate pace over the blue, pink and black spots. If the cue-ball comes back over those

'All players have to learn the hard way about potting angles, and the important thing for the newcomer is to avoid frustration.'

same spots, after it has rebounded off the top cushion, you are OK.

If, however, the cue-ball does not return over the spots but comes back to either the left or the right, you have a problem. The cue-ball strays from its intended course because the player, by hitting diagonally across the white, imparts unintentional sidespin.

There are a number of different causes for this. They include a weak bridge, alignment defects, incorrect grip or poor stance. By making minor adjustments to the problem areas, a player can chart his progress by playing this shot down the spots on a regular basis.

Although I've used this exercise on occasions to give myself peace of mind, it has never played a massive role in my overall practice routine. I'm told, though, that Fred Davis, a former world champion, played this shot a thousand

One test of the straightness of your cueing is to strike the cue-ball down over the brown, blue, pink and black spots and see if it returns down the same line after hitting the top cushion.

times over to groove his cue-action.

After sorting out the technicalities, you can move on to practicalities – specifically how best to practise and hone your potting skills. If you are a newcomer to the game, benefit can be gained from setting up potting situations and knocking in pots from a variety of angles and distances. Obviously, if you consistently fail on one particular type of pot, you need to continue to practise it until your success rate improves.

The line up, a practice exercise leading professionals undertake daily, combines potting and positional skills. The colours are placed on their normal spots, the reds are placed in a line down the middle

> **'After sorting out the technicalities of potting, you can move on to practicalities.'**

of the table, and the object is to compile as big a break as possible.

For pure potting the following routine is more useful. Place five or six reds in a line across the table approximately a foot away from the baulk line. Place the cue-ball on the baulk line, making the pots dead straight and thus forcing the player to make a full-ball contact to pot it.

Aim the cue at the back of the distant pocket into which you hope to pot the object-ball. If you miss, stay down on the shot. If the cue-tip is not pointing directly at the back of the pocket after the follow through, but to the left or right, it is clear that your cueing is not 100 per cent straight.

If, from a foot, you are satisfied with the proportion of shots you are potting, try moving the reds a little further down the table away from the baulk line. The greater the distance between cue-ball and object-ball, the greater is

TESTING YOUR CUE-ACTION

● Frank Callan, one of the leading snooker coaches in Britain and a man whose guidance has been of enormous benefit to many advanced players, myself included, believes this exercise often gives a false impression. Frank quite rightly says that, even if the cue-ball is marginally off course on its journey to the top cushion, it will return along the path of the spots if there is some sidespin applied. This, of course, is true, but if a chalk mark is made on the top cushion to indicate where the cue-ball should make contact, this problem is solved.

Frank has another exercise to discover any deficiency in cue-action: cueing along the baulk line at an imaginary white.

If you are cueing straight, it follows that the cue will obscure the baulk line as the player looks. If the cue at follow through is to the left or right of the baulk line, the player is striking across, instead of straight through, the cue-ball. If the cue has a tendency to slide to the left of the line for a right-hander, it suggests that the thumb of the bridge hand is too high and vice versa. The over-the-spots shot and cueing at a non-existent white may seem the ultimate turn-offs, but solo practice has underpinned the success of all great individual sporting champions. Snooker is no exception.

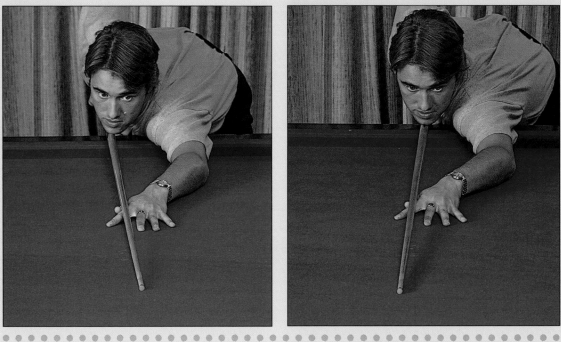

The line up – undoubtedly the most commonly used practice exercise in the game.

the test of a player's cueing. Remember as well that all pots are not straight. Try out other angles and let your mistakes work for you. If you undercut or overcut a pot, register what reaction you get and make the necessary compensation next time around.

'Be prepared to put in some solo practice. At any club you will see the most dedicated members engaged in this solitary ritual.'

Be prepared, too, to put in some solo practice. At any club you will see the most dedicated members engaged in this solitary ritual. In my experience, having seen many youngsters make rapid strides at the John Spencer Snooker Club in Stirling – my practice base – I can say with confidence that, almost without exception, solo practice accelerates improvement and therefore increases the enjoyment of the beginner.

THE EFFECT OF THE NAP

After a few frames, even the most unobservant of you will have noticed that the green cloth that provides the table's surface has a definite pile. This is called the nap.

It is like that of a carpet and runs all

The best exercise for pure potting improvement: try to pot as many of these long, straight reds as you can. Of course, the potting angles you set yourself are up to you.

the same way – from the baulk end to the top cushion. Consequently, up the table is with the nap while down the table towards baulk is against the nap. It has a significant effect on the travel of the cue-ball, especially across the table and at a slow pace.

Sometimes when visiting your local snooker club you will hear, and maybe even utter, howls of disbelief when a ball, which has apparently been contacted perfectly, fails to enter a pocket because it has rolled off – i.e. deviated – from a straight course.

Playing conditions are not ideal on every table and a 'crook' table can sometimes rob you of a pot. While this is frustrating, there is little a player can do to avoid it other than stroke the object-ball harder. However, when players walk away from a level table and moan about a ball rolling off, it is probably the effects of the nap which cause the pot to be missed.

The nap consists of millions of minute fibres all lying in the same direction. Stroke it from the baulk end to the top cushion and it feels smooth. The other way you can feel resistance. That is because the nap's fibres act as a force trying to pull balls played down the table back to the top cushion. It is obvious that this pulling effect will be more pronounced the slower the pace of the shot concerned.

In terms of potting, the nap comes into play most when you are potting a ball into either middle pocket from the top end (black spot) of the table. If you place a red on the pink spot and attempt to pot it to a middle pocket at a quiet pace, you will see the nap at work.

Assuming that the shot is rolled, as opposed to punched, the red will turn away from the pocket on the low side (see diagram). In order to avoid hitting the nearside jaw, one has to aim for the far jaw rather than the middle of the pocket. The amount of deviation is directly related to the heaviness of the cloth.

The nap does not only affect pots into the middle pockets. As the nap always pulls the ball towards the top cushion, a pot across the top cushion is easier to complete than one across the baulk cushion. Balls struck across the baulk cushion tend to wander away, while a ball played across the top cushion tends to cling. Bear this in mind when you are faced with the choice of taking on one of these pots or settling for safety.

When attempting to pot a red from the pink spot, you will see the effect of the nap. If the shot is rolled, as opposed to punched, the red will turn away from the pocket on the low side.

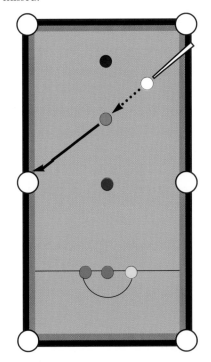

THE TABLES WE PROFESSIONALS PLAY ON IN MAJOR TOURNAMENTS HAVE SUPER-FINE MATCH CLOTHS WITH LITTLE NAP. IT TOOK ME A WHILE TO GET USED TO NOT ALLOWING FOR SOME SURFACE SWING WHEN PLAYING SLOW-PACED SHOTS INTO THE MIDDLE POCKETS. THESE SUPER-FINE CLOTHS ARE RESPONSIVE AND A DELIGHT TO PLAY ON, BUT THEY ARE HARDLY IDEAL FOR THE CONSTANT WEAR AND TEAR THEY WOULD RECEIVE IN CLUBS. AS A RESULT OF THIS, MOST CLUB TABLES ARE COVERED WITH THICKER, MORE HEAVY-DUTY CLOTHS WHICH NATURALLY HAVE STRONGER NAPS.

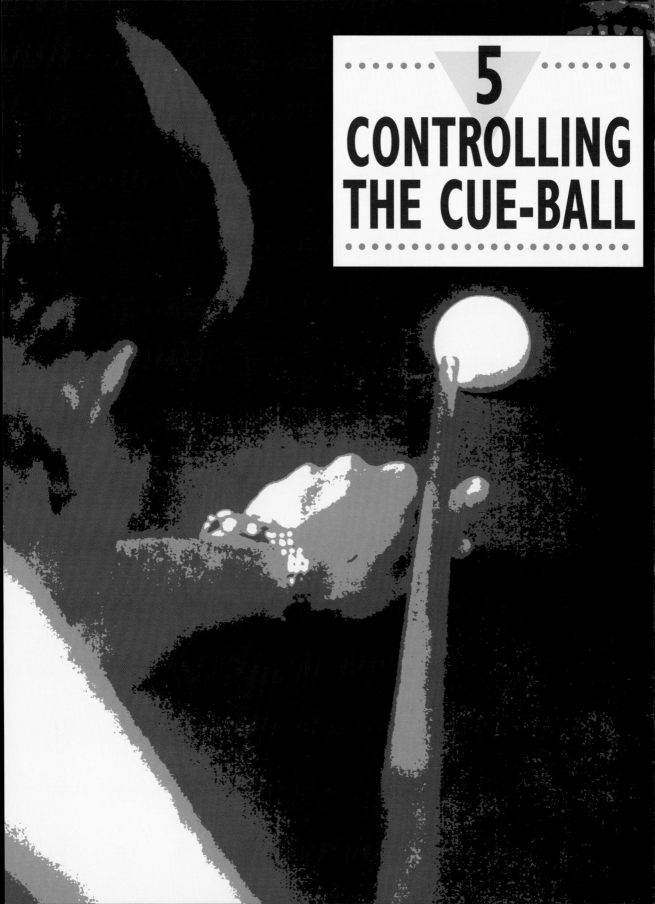

5
CONTROLLING THE CUE-BALL

When you first take up the game, potting will occupy so much of your attention that you may not be able to contemplate positional play. After a short while, though, you will begin to realise the importance of manoeuvring the cue-ball and controlling it for your own benefit.

As yet, no one has been such an effective potter that he is able to disregard positional play and still compete at a high level, though there are, of course, players whose potting is better than their positional play and vice versa. Obviously there is no point in sacrificing a pot in order to obtain inch perfect position on your next ball, but the easier you make your next shot, the greater the likelihood that you will pot it. A sizeable break always contains a sequence of easy pots made possible by deft, accurate cue-ball control.

'The easier you make your next shot, the greater the likelihood that you will pot it.'

The major problem in playing a positional shot is a split in concentration between potting the object-ball and obtaining the desired position. It's a bit like a circus performer riding a unicycle and juggling at the same time. For the novice, the best advice I can give is not to run before you can walk. If you feel that concentrating on position will significantly reduce your chances of potting a ball, forget about position. However, as you gain more experience, you must begin to develop some positional skills. The same applies for positional play.

I wish I had a pound for every time I've heard a player say, 'Why didn't I just knock that red in? I was thinking too much about getting on the blue,' or something along those lines. It would be equal to winning a tournament.

The key is to learn from experience. Try to devote an appropriate proportion of your concentration to the two aspects of a shot, and always bear in mind that the pot is of paramount importance. Miss it, attain ideal position and your opponent is presented with a scoring opportunity. Pot it and run out of position and at least you've got the option to play safe. This might sound a negative way to think, but it's sensible sometimes. Of course, if you always think this way, you will never improve. If you're practising by yourself or with a friend of your own standard, what does it matter if you miss through attempting to play to a higher standard? Try to push back the boundaries of your limitations gradually. If your lifetime highest break is 25, it's too early to try to play Jimmy White.

REMEMBER:

1. Don't sacrifice a pot for positional requirements.
2. Don't run before you can walk.
3. Devote the appropriate proportion of your concentration to all aspects of the shot.

TYPES OF CUE-BALL CONTROL

The cue-ball is manoeuvred into its desired position by a player imparting various forms of spin. This spin is achieved by striking the cue-ball at different points on its face. Three basic forms of spin can be generated: topspin, sidespin and backspin.

Topspin

When explaining topspin, it is best to think of the surface of the white as a clock face. To apply topspin, or overspin, the white should be struck at twelve o'clock. By doing that, a player will

Topspin, follow through on the white, is generated by raising the bridge hand so that the cue runs through the white, as horizontally as possible, at twelve o'clock.

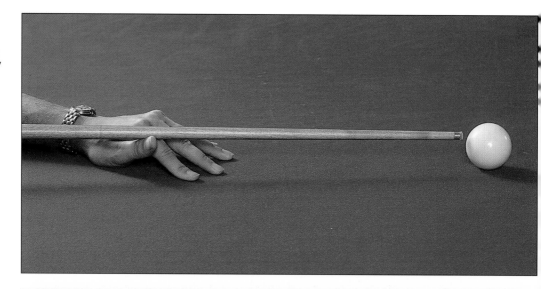

Hitting down on to the top of the cue-ball has the effect only of imparting an unwanted masse-type spin.

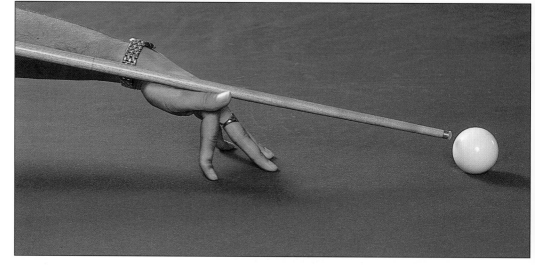

cause the cue-ball to follow through once it has made contact with the object-ball.

If you place the blue on its spot and the cue-ball some six inches directly behind it, leaving a dead straight pot into the middle pocket, the white follows the blue in if enough topspin and, of course, pace are used.

To generate maximum follow through and genuine topspin, it is no good strik-

ing down on the cue-ball. As striking above centre on the white is required, a player must raise his bridge just enough to allow this to happen, with the cue running parallel to the surface of the table at the same time.

Backspin

As backspin is the polar opposite to topspin, its application is achieved by striking the cue-ball below centre. The cue-ball will, after making contact with the object-ball, spin back or stop dead. The exact reaction depends on a number of variables, which include where the cue-tip strikes the white, the angle of contact between the cue-ball and object-ball and also the original distance between them.

Before I go into the workings of backspin, I must impress on you the importance of chalking your cue before playing a stun or screw shot. Chalk on the tip allows it to grip the white when the shot is made. Without chalk, the white slides off the tip and the likelihood of a miscue increases dramatically.

With the stun shot, the cue-tip strikes the white marginally below centre. This causes only a small amount of backspin to be imparted, just sufficient, in fact, to stop the cue-ball dead if it is making a full-ball contact with the object-ball. As most shots are not straight, this happens only occasionally.

The main positional benefit of the stun shot is that, when playing an angled pot, it allows a player to send the cue-ball off the object-ball at a variety of angles. The actual angle depends on the amount of stun effect imparted on to the white.

'I must impress on you the importance of chalking your cue before playing a stun or screw shot.'

If you continue to think of the cue-ball as a clock face, then a player gets more screw effect, i.e. backspin, as the point of contact between tip and white moves towards six o'clock. For some reason a deep screw shot – where the white is screwed back a long distance – excites the snooker-watching public more than

CUE-POWER

PEOPLE OFTEN ASK ME WHO HAS THE MOST CUE-POWER IN THE PROFESSIONAL GAME. JOHN SPENCER, WORLD CHAMPION IN 1969, 1970 AND 1977, AND CANADA'S BILL WERBENIUK WERE ALWAYS GREAT EXPONENTS OF THE SCREW SHOT, AS WAS ALEX HIGGINS.

OF THE CURRENT TOP-LEVEL PLAYERS, NEAL FOULDS (RIGHT) STANDS HEAD AND SHOULDERS ABOVE THE REST OF US BECAUSE HIS CUE ACTION ALLOWS HIM TO GO FREELY THROUGH THE WHITE. NEAL CAN QUITE EASILY SCREW BACK INTO BAULK FROM A RED LEVEL WITH THE BLACK SPOT. I'M HAPPY WITH MY OWN CUE POWER, AS I'M SURE MOST OF THE TOP PLAYERS ARE. ONLY ONE, JAMES WATTANA, FALLS SHORT OF POSSESSING TRUE POWER, BUT HIS EXCEPTIONAL TOUCH AND FEEL FOR A SHOT MAKE UP FOR IT.

anything else. Perhaps this is because of the power involved or because of the spectacular nature of the shot. Perhaps it is, but I tend to support another theory.

Many players, as a result of their own technical weaknesses, find it difficult – if not impossible – to screw a ball back more than a couple of inches. To these people the sight of Jimmy White, Alan McManus or John Parrott screwing the cue-ball back huge distances is like watching a magician perform his best trick. Yet, while skill obviously plays a major part, there is nothing to prevent any player becoming proficient with backspin.

'The success of a screw shot depends on timing rather than raw power.'

The white does not come back by magic. A ball with topspin begins its forward motion as soon as the cue-tip comes into contact with it. When the cue-ball contacts the object-ball, it stops rolling for a fraction of a second before its forward momentum reasserts itself and it follows through. When deep screw is imparted, there is a totally different reaction. After tip and cue-ball have come into contact, the white skids towards the object-ball. It is resisting forward movement, so when it eventually makes contact with the object-ball, which is obviously stationary, the collision helps the white to push back.

When it comes to the actual playing of the shot itself, a number of fundamental technical requirements need to be fulfilled in order for there to be a successful outcome. After making long, smoother preliminary addresses at the cue-ball – watch Neal Foulds – always remember to let your cue do the work on the shot. It is also vital that your cue should be at maximum acceleration as it strikes the white and that you make sure to follow through. In this sense, it is like a bunker shot in golf.

The success of a screw shot depends on timing rather than raw power. That means rhythm is important, so jerky, disjointed waggles and fierce cue grips are

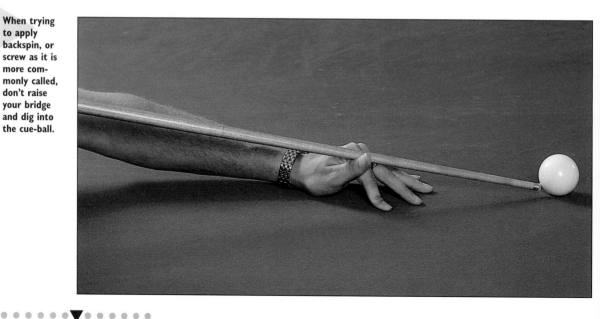

When trying to apply backspin, or screw as it is more commonly called, don't raise your bridge and dig into the cue-ball.

Screw is best applied by lowering the bridge so that the cue runs through the white at a horizontal plane.

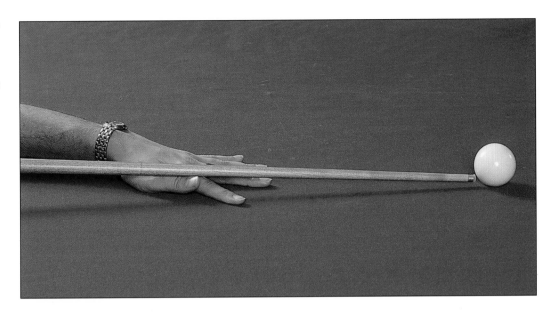

to be discouraged. The basic guidelines of cue-action – elimination of upper-body, shoulder and head movement – should also apply.

Without doubt, however, the most common mistake committed by players having problems with the application of backspin is striking down at the cue-ball. For topspin a player should raise his bridge to keep his cue as horizontal as possible to the surface of the table. This principle, in reverse, holds true for back-spin.

When playing a screw shot, simply lower the bridge so that the cue is run-ning on a horizontal plane as it strikes the white at six o'clock. Otherwise your ability to apply backspin will be severely limited and, with your 'scooping' cue action, you will be bedevilled by miscues and jump shots.

When I play a match of any length, with an average number of scoring visits included, it would be a conservative estimate to say that 70 per cent of my positional shots incorporate the use of stun or screw. To play to a high standard,

therefore, these shots must be mastered.

Traditionally the practice exercise used by beginners attempting to develop a knowledge of screw shots has involved the blue being placed on its spot, with the cue-ball, in a straight line, some six inches behind it.

The idea is to pot the blue into the facing mid-dle pocket and screw the cue-ball back into the middle pocket

'To play to a high standard, stun and screw shots must be mastered.'

nearest the player. However, this exercise has a drawback because the backspin applied to the white screws it back quickly, forcing a player to remove his cue and bridge hand even more swiftly in order to avoid making contact with them. There will therefore be a tenden-cy for the player, knowing subconscious-ly what will happen, not to complete his follow through fully. This follow through is vital if the screw shot is to be success-ful. A jabbing action does not work.

PRACTISING THE SCREW SHOT

● A practice exercise which does not interfere with a player's follow through is now more widely employed by top coaches. Place the white on the baulk line and a red twelve inches up the table towards the top cushion. Here the pot is not of paramount importance. First learn to screw the white over the baulk line. When you have done this, move the red further and further away from the baulk line. You will soon discover that the greater the distance between cue-ball and object-ball, the harder it is to apply screw effect. This is because spin is lost from the cue-ball the further it has to travel. A screw shot with the cue-ball and object-ball nine inches apart is easy to execute, because when contact is made a high percentage of the originally imparted backspin still remains.

If, however, the cue-ball has to travel, say, five feet, much of the backspin has disappeared by the time contact is made with the object-ball. Consequently, entirely different reactions occur over a range of distances. If the cue-ball was struck in such a way as to impart *x* amount of backspin, it could produce a deep screw effect off an object-ball twelve inches away and a stun effect off an object-ball five feet away.

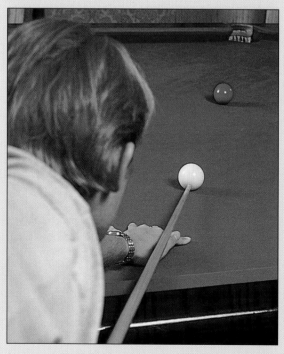

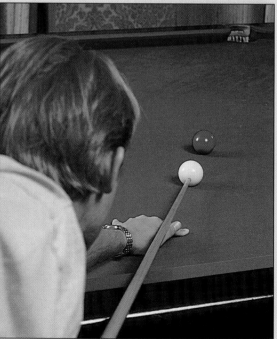

As these photographs show, I have to strike the cue-ball lower for a stun shot the further apart the white and object-ball are.

The Stun Run Through Shot

On the overwhelming majority of occasions, this shot is used when a player is faced with a pot which is straight or just off straight. This shot, which allows a player to hit the cue-ball with power, is a 'feel' shot and is difficult to perfect.

Basically, when stun run through effect is successfully applied, the cue-ball checks up for a fraction of a second before running through for a short distance. Even the most inexperienced player reading this will probably be thinking, 'There's no need for this shot; you can get the same effect by playing a slow-paced shot with topspin.' Of course this is correct, but there are two reasons why a slow dribble should be avoided when an alternative is available.

'The most difficult aspect of positional play for anyone to master is the application of sidespin.'

Firstly, most players find it easier to retain a straight cue-action delivery if they are striking the cue-ball firmly. Also, by rolling in pots, a player leaves himself open to the possibility of the object-ball leaving its true course because of table conditions.

Professionals, for the most part, are cosseted, playing on excellent tables under virtually ideal and very consistent conditions. However, even our tables run off slightly on occasions. All tables do and you should be ready for it – which is why having a stun run shot in your armoury is invaluable.

A player has to discover by trial and error where to strike the cue-ball. Feel plays a part in the equation, as does the distance between cue-ball and object-ball. The perfect spot for the cue-tip to make contact with the white can be dis-

covered only by practice. If you strike the cue-ball too high it will follow through too much, while too low a strike has the opposite effect of checking up the cue-ball. It is a thin dividing line between success and failure, even for the leading players.

Sidespin

I can say with confidence that the most difficult aspect of positional play for anyone to master is the application of sidespin. Come to think of it, the use of side causes more than its share of problems even for the best professionals.

Steve Davis has always maintained that it is unwise to employ side unless it is absolutely necessary, and nothing in my experience leads me to disagree. Its use is fraught with danger as it makes potting more difficult, in most instances at least, and there's no getting away from how difficult using it can be for beginners; but when a shot goes astray, it pays to bear in mind the benefits to all aspects of a player's game if it is used properly and accurately. Like screw and stun shots, side plays a huge role in the modern game, both in terms of safety play and break-building.

As with screw, stun and topspin shots, there is a right and wrong way to apply side. The most important thing to remember is that the cue strikes the edges of the white without being delivered diagonally. Glancing blows are not effective – take it from me

THE APPLICATION OF SIDE IS SO COMPLICATED THAT IT CAN CREATE UNTOLD HEADACHES FOR EVEN THE GAME'S GREATEST PLAYERS. UNWANTED AND CONSISTENT GENERATION OF SIDESPIN ON VIRTUALLY EVERY SHOT HAS LED TO LONG PERIODS OF FRUSTRATION FOR TWO FORMER WORLD CHAMPIONS, STEVE DAVIS AND CLIFF THORBURN. BOTH HAVE NOW CURED THE PROBLEM OF UNINTENTIONALLY APPLYING SIDESPIN BUT FOR SOME TIME DAVIS WAS PUTTING RIGHT-HAND SIDE ON ALMOST EVERY SHOT BY CUEING ACROSS THE WHITE AND THORBURN WAS DOING LIKEWISE WITH LEFT-HAND SIDE.

WHAT IS SIDE AND HOW IS IT APPLIED?

● **Side is applied by a player's cue-tip making contact with either the left or right-hand side of the white. Assuming the cue-ball is struck at nine o'clock (with right-hand side), its path is as follows (see diagram).**

The white initially pushes to the left before the right-hand sidespin begins to bite and causes the cue-ball to curl back to the right. The effect of side is most pronounced when the white hits a cushion. If right-hand side has been imparted, it rebounds to the right of the natural angle. Apart from the obvious two forms of side – left and right – there is check side and running side. Left-hand side may be check in one instance, running side in another.

Running side has the effect of widening the angle at which the cue-ball leaves the cushion and increasing the travelling distance of the white. Conversely, check side narrows the angle the cue-ball takes off a cushion as well as reducing its run. It is these unnatural reactions off a cushion that allow a player to manoeuvre the cue-ball in a way which maximises positional efficiency.

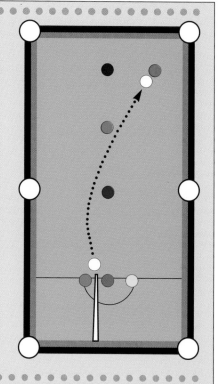

– so to avoid them a player should not address the cue-ball in the centre and then strike across it to the left or right.

If you want to use right-hand side, address the white at the point of contact so that your cueing will be along a straight line and not a diagonal one. This solid cueing through the ball acts to generate far more controllable sidespin than a glancing blow, which increases the likelihood of a miscue.

'By trial and error, you can develop the ability to make the necessary adjustments when using side.'

What makes potting more difficult when using side is the fact that side operates off object-balls as well as off cushions – creating the need for plain-ball sighting to be readjusted accordingly.

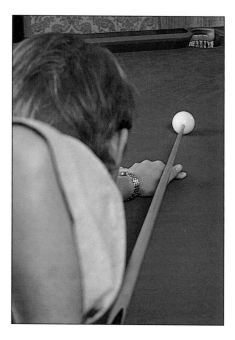

This shows a simple plain-ball cue-tip contact with the white.

You will successfully apply right-hand side if, like in this shot, you address the right-hand side of the cue-ball and cue through it in a straight line.

The same principle applies, of course, if you are trying to impart left-hand side (my stance would not normally be like this; I am upright only to allow the camera to see how I am striking the cue-ball).

Many amateurs try to apply sidespin by cueing across the white.

Glancing blows increase the likelihood of a miscue and they don't work.

Check side causes the object-ball to 'straighten' up after it has made contact with the cue-ball. Therefore a contact that would lead to a successful pot if the white had been hit 'plain-ball' (without side) would cause the object-ball to be undercut if check side had been applied.

On the other hand, a shot played with running side would lead to the object-ball being overcut if plain-ball alignment was adopted. A player, by trial and error, gradually develops the ability to make the necessary sighting adjustments when using side, or he continues to use 'plain-ball' alignment for shots with side and pays a heavy penalty.

With so many pitfalls associated with the use of side when potting, you may wonder why it is used at all. A few successfully executed positional shots will show you the reason why. The correct application of side is like a passport, allowing the cue-ball to reach parts of the table off certain shots that would be impossible with exclusively plain-ball striking.

Swerve Shots

The most extreme application of side can be seen in a swerve shot. Like a deep screw shot these, played properly, are spectacular and most players wish to master them.

Swerve shots are most useful when a player has to escape from a snooker, for the excessive amount of spin imparted causes the cue-ball to travel in an arc, thus allowing a player to extract himself from a snooker without hitting a cushion. Obviously, with a certain amount of practice, most players can impart the necessary spin to make the cue-ball swerve. The key is to be able to control the level of swerve.

'Only with time and experience does your standard of positional play improve.'

The cue-ball swerves around any intervening balls as a result of the effect of sidespin. To apply this spin it is necessary to raise the butt of the cue well above the horizontal. The higher one raises the butt of the cue, the more spin – and therefore swerve – it is possible to apply.

If only a small amount of swerve is required, a player could impart sufficient side by adopting a normal bridge. However, more dramatic swerves require the butt to be raised to around forty-five degrees, so that the cue-tip strikes a downward blow on the white.

Raising the butt means lifting the bridge, so that the heel of the hand is off the table and supported solely by the fingertips. If you raise the bridge near the vertical, it is possible to apply extreme amounts of spin. I can almost get the cue-ball to complete a semicircle. This is known as the massé shot.

For a swerve shot, the cue must strike the white sharply but with little or no follow through. The cue-tip, which must strike the white with both power and authority, must bite into the cue-ball in order to apply the left or right-hand side required. If a player hits the cue-ball too softly, not enough spin effect will be generated for the white to swerve.

This shot, while of great help in escaping snookers, is of very limited use in potting. Only when the ball 'on' is over a pocket can a player attempt a swerve pot with any degree of confidence. Whenever you see a player pot a ball with a swerve from other positions, it is usually more by luck than judgement.

Cue-ball control is a vital cog in a winning snooker machine. It is not easy, so don't expect things to fall into place overnight. You must work, practise and experiment with certain shots. I once lost a frame because I played a pot with bundles of check side which went astray. Afterwards I was angry with myself, but once I had time to settle down I realised it was the only way to learn about that particular shot. Only with time and experience does your standard of positional play improve. One thing is for sure: when it does improve, a player gains tremendous satisfaction and has a better chance of being a consistent winner of frames.

PLAYING CONDITIONS

● So far you could easily get the misleading impression that topspin, screw and stun, sidespin and swerve shots yield a consistent reaction on all tables. This could not be further from the truth, as playing conditions, which vary greatly from table to table, often determine the positional capabilities of a player.

If the cushions are slow and unresponsive or the bed of the table is sluggish, certain positional shots become difficult or even impossible. The same holds true with tight pockets. On one table a pot may be relatively easy, while on another, because of the tightness of its pockets, it becomes an extremely tough proposition.

If you complain about a table, people who do not understand the problem often think it is a case of sour grapes. It's certainly true that some things are all the same – such as the dimensions of the playing surface, the colour of the cloth and the position of the spots – and weather problems are not the factor that they are in many other sports. However, after you have played on many different tables, you will learn that conditions are anything but uniform. On the most badly maintained tables, beer stains, oily patches and even rips can cause problems, but the biggest factor is the overall state of the cloth.

If a table has a heavy cloth, it will be slow-running, screw and stun will be easy to apply and the effects of sidespin will be exaggerated. If, in contrast, the table is bald, the pace of the cloth will guarantee that it is hard to control the cue-ball. Because the spin has nothing to 'bite' on, deep screw shots become virtually unplayable.

These poor conditions can drive a player to frustration, and a bad table is a great leveller, as a player with a wide range of advanced shots is unable to use them. It is not unlike Brazil, Argentina or any of the world's most powerful footballing nations finding it difficult to beat a third-rate club side because they are unable to display their superior soccer skills on a pitch in the middle of a ploughed field.

A player's ability to wrestle with these assorted problems lies in his mental approach. He must become aware of his limitations and, more importantly, the limitations imposed on him by the table. Countless players have lost matches on strange tables, to opponents of inferior ability, because they have not adapted to prevailing playing conditions. I know because in my youth it happened to me.

You have probably noticed that in my press conferences I very rarely moan about a particular table, but that isn't to say I'm happy with bad conditions. When I lost 5-2 to Dave Harold on an outside table in the last 16 of the 1993 Asian Open, the conditions were of a low standard because of air conditioning in the hotel venue.

I played very badly, but didn't mention this afterwards because the fact was simply that Dave had adapted better than I. In fact, Dave adapted to the damp cloths better than anyone, going on to win the title and making a 137 total clearance against Darren Morgan in the final.

The complete beginner starts to realise, after playing only a few frames, that the cue-ball is not always in position to employ the normal bridge or stance. The basic techniques become impossible to use and have to be temporarily abandoned.

This happens when the cue-ball is either under or close to a cushion, when it is in close proximity to another ball, or when it's beyond a player's normal reach.

To counteract these awkward positions, other types of supplementary bridges and stances have been developed and the player also has a variety of rests available.

SUPPLEMENTARY BRIDGES

The game would be far simpler if a player could use the orthodox bridge for every shot. However, certain finishing positions of the cue-ball make it necessary for a player to learn the bridge

PLAYING FROM UNDER A CUSHION

● If you find yourself with the cue-ball tucked under the side-cushion, don't panic, but make some technical adjustments. If you don't attempt to do too much with the cue-ball, there's nothing to stop you completing the shot with success. It was once maintained that this shot is best played with fingers flat on the cushion rail, thus keeping the cue's delivery as horizontal as possible. Now the cushion bridge, in which the bridge-hand is slightly raised and the wrist dropped below the level of the cushion, is more in vogue. It is certainly the one I tend to favour in such situations.

This cushion bridge allows more flexibility, although it does have the disadvantage of forcing a player to strike the cue-ball a downward blow, thus significantly increasing the chance of a degree of unwanted sidespin being applied. With positions where the cue-ball is just a few inches off the cushion, don't try to place your bridge-hand on the cloth as normal. If you do, you will be cramped up and, as a result, the rhythm and straightness of your cue-action could be seriously compromised.

The looped bridge is sometimes used for this kind of shot. Here the fingertips rest on the green baize part of the cushion rail, while the heel of the hand is in contact with the wood. With this bridge a player does not cock his thumb. Instead, the thumb should be moved under the forefinger so that it is touching the joint of the middle finger. After the forefinger has been looped around the cue the inside of the forefinger and the outside of the middle finger form the channel that guides the cue on delivery. I do not use this bridge very frequently, but those players who are confident with it are generally able to play power shots more effectively.

With a cue-ball right under the cushion, I place my fingers on the cushion rail and concentrate on avoiding a downward blow to the white.

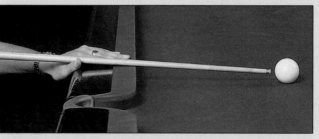

With the cue-ball just off the cushion, this is my preferred bridge.

In this situation a lot of players find that the looped bridge gives them more confidence.

For an elevated bridge, lift the hand, spread your fingers widely and press the fingers into the cloth to make the bridge solid.

As you can see from this, it is important that the bridge should be as close as it can be to the intervening ball to help your sighting of the shot.

best suited for a particular shot.

The most common of these tricky positions occurs when the cue-ball has come to rest under a cushion. Even the very best professionals do not feel comfortable in such a situation and many dread playing this kind of shot at a tense stage of a match. Despite winning six world titles between 1970 and 1978, Ray Reardon found great difficulty in potting from under the cushion. One of the keys to breakbuilding is therefore the ability to manoeuvre the cue-ball into positions which allow the normal bridge to be used.

Cushions do not provide the only bridging problem. When a shot has to be played with intervening balls blocking the path to the cue-ball, bridging can become extremely difficult. To give the cue the necessary elevation to strike

down on the obscured white, the bridge hand has to be raised.

After lifting the hand, spread the fingers widely and press them into the cloth so that the bridge has maximum stability. Obviously the height of the bridge depends entirely on how near the intervening ball is to the cue-ball. If the white is almost directly behind another ball, then a near-vertical bridge is required. As the distance between cue-ball and the ball obstructing it widens, the cue, and therefore the bridge-hand, do not need such a steep angle of elevation.

'One of the keys to break-building is the ability to manoeuvre the cue-ball into positions which allow the normal bridge to be used.'

THREE-FINGER BRIDGE

MOST PLAYERS, ESPECIALLY THOSE WITH SHORT FINGERS, FIND IT DIFFICULT TO MAKE AN ELEVATED BRIDGE WITH ALL FOUR FINGERS ON THE BED OF THE TABLE. DENNIS TAYLOR, THE 1985 WORLD CHAMPION, OFTEN EMPLOYS A TWO- OR THREE-FINGER BRIDGE IN THESE SITUATIONS. HE TELLS ME HE FEELS MORE COMFORTABLE DOING THAT AND HE FEELS THE STABILITY OF THE BRIDGE IS NOT ADVERSELY AFFECTED.

The bridge should always be placed as near as possible to the intervening ball so that sighting, which is arguably the hardest aspect of these shots, is made as easy as possible.

Some players, particularly novices, are petrified when faced with the prospect of having to play one of these shots. It is important to banish all negative thoughts and approach the shot with confidence. Always bear in mind that, by adopting a technically sound bridge, a player can attain an adequate level of consistency.

Don't try anything too intricate, but keep the stroke as simple as you can, strike the cue-ball – don't stab into it – and, above all else, concentrate your attention on keeping as still as you can on the shot.

SUPPLEMENTARY STANCES

It is in the rules that a player must keep at least some part of one foot on the floor while a shot is being played. Sometimes it is possible to avoid the use of the rest by lifting one leg off the ground, sometimes resting it on the cushion rail, or even on the actual surface of the table itself. The great advantage of this stance is that it allows the player to use his normal bridge.

Being able to rest one leg on the table can often help you avoid having to use the rest. This can be a big advantage.

Next time you are playing snooker in a room with a number of tables, just take time to notice how many people over-stretch and miss relatively simple pots as a result of their makeshift, unsteady stance. Whenever possible, try to place your back leg on the table so that it takes your weight. With your front leg touching the floor, this solid stance must improve your chances of completing the shot successfully. If this is not possible, do not overreach with your back leg waving up and down and your cue delivery anything but straight.

USING THE REST

Children who take up the game at an early age tend to become competent rest players because, with their short reach, they frequently need to use it, while older beginners are often frightened by the rest. John Spencer and Dennis Taylor, both former world champions,

and Malta's Tony Drago are among those who admit that their rest play has been a weakness throughout their careers. Taylor, no doubt conscious of this weakness, can play a wide range of shots left-handed – but he is an exception. Others soldier on, making plenty of 'rest' mistakes and consequently losing frames they should have won.

When playing with the rest, the orthodox grip and stance are

'Players often overstretch and miss relatively simple pots as a result of their makeshift, unsteady stance.'

not used. The cue is held at the end of the butt, something like the way one would hold a pen, with the thumb providing support underneath and two fingers placed on top. The hand (the left for a right-hander) which usually makes the bridge had another function this

● So what makes a good rest player? The most common technical fault amongst novices is to use the rest tall way up. It is always preferable to use the shallow V because it allows a cue, running horizontal to the bed of the table, to strike the white virtually dead centre. Using the rest tall way up leads to the cue striking downward into the cue-ball. Obviously, when the white has to be hit between eleven o'clock and one o'clock to impart topspin, tall way up is fine – otherwise it is to be avoided.

The actual rest makes a big difference to your success rate with the shot as well. I despise plastic rests because they are so light and flimsy that it is extremely hard to control them. Metal-headed rests are much better, as they give a player far greater stability. Similarly a rest with a tight V head is far better than one with a U-shaped head which will cause the cue to wobble during delivery.

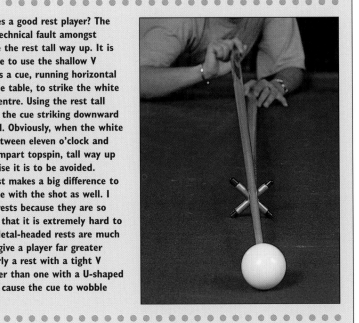

The grip for using the rest is like someone holding a pen with the thumb underneath the cue for support. The other hand is used to anchor the rest to the table.

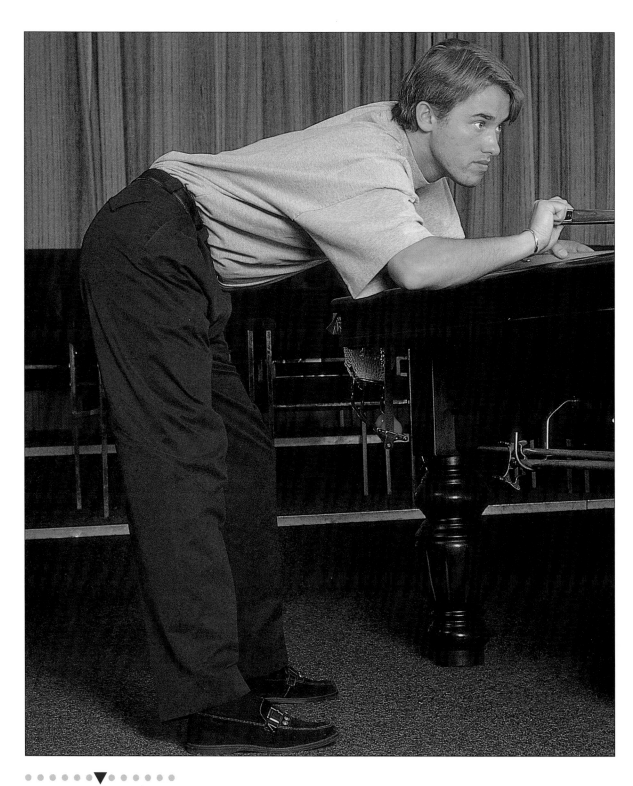

time, being employed to anchor the rest firmly to the table.

Some players hold the rest butt in the air but, unless this is the only option because of the awkward position of balls on the table, it is not recommended. By securing the rest to the table with your free hand, you greatly improve the general stability on the shot.

The stance, like the grip, bears very little resemblance to that adopted under normal circumstances. When it is possible to use the orthodox bridge, the cue-arm and cue go through the white in a direct line. With the rest, the elbow swings sideways to the cue, even though the cue itself is pushed through straight.

In order to do this, your stance has to be modified so that you are virtually side-on. It is a help to straight cueing if the elbow of the cue-arm is dipped marginally to

allow the arm to be horizontal to the table. The cue is best held just below eye level so that the cue, and sometimes the butt of the rest, can assist alignment.

The cue-action tends to be a push of the forearm and wrist, rather than a flowing movement. At all times upper body movement should be reduced to a minimum and the actual delivery of the cue, as well as the important preliminary

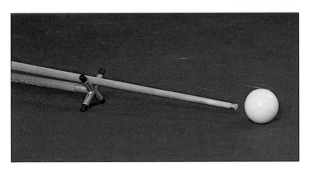

'With patience and skill, it is possible to have almost as full a range of shots with the rest as it is with the normal bridge.'

addresses to the cue-ball, should be made as smoothly and rhythmically as possible. Unless intervening balls render it impossible, the rest-head should be placed six to eight inches from the white, as it is with a player's bridge under normal circumstances.

I have already explained the perils of being over-ambitious when faced with a shot from under a cushion or over intervening balls. The same warning, slightly watered down, applies to the rest. An example of a shot which needs to be played with caution is a deep screw.

Remember screw shots are played most effectively when a player lowers his bridge to allow the cue to run as horizontally as possible to the bed of the table. As the rest head is fixed, it cannot be lowered, and you therefore have to strike the cue-ball a downward blow to impart the necessary backspin. Inevitably the likelihood of a 'scooping' miscue dramatically increases.

These are just cautionary warnings and are not in any way designed to deter a player from playing anything other than the most straightforward, plain-ball shot with the rest. At first it is difficult to master but, with patience and skill, it is possible to have almost as full a range of shots with the rest as it is with the normal bridge.

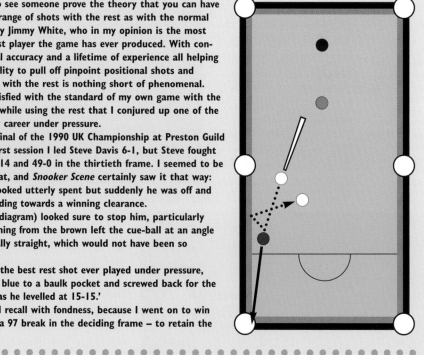

● If you want to see someone prove the theory that you can have almost as full a range of shots with the rest as with the normal bridge, just study Jimmy White, who in my opinion is the most accomplished rest player the game has ever produced. With confidence, technical accuracy and a lifetime of experience all helping him, Jimmy's ability to pull off pinpoint positional shots and spectacular pots with the rest is nothing short of phenomenal.

I'm pretty satisfied with the standard of my own game with the rest, and it was while using the rest that I conjured up one of the best shots of my career under pressure.

It was in the final of the 1990 UK Championship at Preston Guild Hall. After the first session I led Steve Davis 6-1, but Steve fought back to lead 15-14 and 49-0 in the thirtieth frame. I seemed to be heading for defeat, and *Snooker Scene* certainly saw it that way:

'. . . Hendry looked utterly spent but suddenly he was off and running and heading towards a winning clearance.

The blue (see diagram) looked sure to stop him, particularly when its positioning from the brown left the cue-ball at an angle instead of virtually straight, which would not have been so difficult a pot.

With possibly the best rest shot ever played under pressure, Hendry sent the blue to a baulk pocket and screwed back for the frame-ball pink as he levelled at 15-15.'

It was a shot I recall with fondness, because I went on to win 16-15 – making a 97 break in the deciding frame – to retain the title.

Even for the world's top players, the half and threequarter-butt rests are a nightmare to use. A cue extension makes things so much easier.

OTHER RESTS

Apart from the conventional rests, there are others known as the half-butt and threequarter-butt. These rests (the half-butt is around 2.8 metres long) come complete with their own cue of the same extended length. They are designed to allow a player to reach shots over the full length of the table and, in this, they fulfil a purpose. However, because of their cumbersome nature, their weight, their instability and, in many cases, their raised heads, these rests are very difficult to use with authority. In recent years these long rests have been all but made redundant at top level by the introduction of the cue extensions discussed earlier.

As you can tell, the spider provides extra elevation to bridge over obstructing balls.

As with the ordinary rest, a side-on stance is used and the rest itself must be anchored to the table with your spare hand.

The final type of rest is called a spider and, as everyone quickly discovers, it is by far the most awkward of the reaching aids to use. The spider, of which there are three basic types, provides the elevation required to bridge over intervening balls that are out of reach. Apart from the normal spider there is an extended spider, which is called into action when more than one ball blocks the path to the cue-ball, and the swan-neck. This affords maximum elevation but, as you might expect, it is also the most difficult to use.

As with the ordinary rest, the butt should be anchored to the bed of the table, as steadiness is absolutely vital for

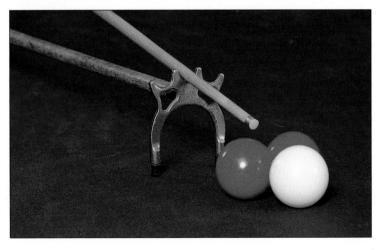

the success of the shot. As you are striking down on the cue-ball when employing these implements, it is all too easy to go widely off the mark. When playing with the spider, always keep it simple and do not put much power into the cue-ball unless absolutely necessary.

The awkwardness of a spider shot is obvious: that's why the best advice is to keep the shot simple.

7
BREAKBUILDING

The size of an amateur's highest break is usually a reliable indicator of his overall standard. Someone who plays on a regular basis and does not boast a run over 40 must either be a poor potter or have serious flaws in the positional side of his game. Those who have topped the 70 break mark are well above average, although there is still plenty of scope for improvement. Those members of the rapidly expanding, century break club can be classified as competent breakbuilders. Breaks of over 100 were once extremely rare at all but the highest level, but over the past twenty years the general standard has improved to such an extent that they are relatively common, even in local leagues and inter-club competitions. Great pleasure and personal satisfaction can be gained from beating your own personal best break.

I can vividly remember making my first century. It was such a satisfying feeling, knowing that I had developed sufficient cue-ball control to be able to reach such a landmark. This is all very well, of course, but the practical purpose of breakbuilding is to win frames. A player can pot and control the cue-ball well, yet still fail to reach his optimum break-building capacity. One needs knowledge of the best shots to play in a given situation, and over the next few pages my aim is to point you in the right direction. Your approach to breakbuilding should then improve.

RED/BLACK BREAKBUILDING

Taking fifteen reds, fifteen blacks and the six colours in sequence is the ultimate in breakbuilding and a feat only a tiny percentage of all snooker players manage during their careers. My first maximum in competition came against Willie Thorne in the 1992 Matchroom League and my second against Jimmy White in the World Championship in 1995. By the end of the 1994-95 season only twenty-one had been compiled in professional events. In everyday situations the black is the most profitable ball around which to construct a break. Because of its value, greater than any other ball on the table, the black enables a player to make a significant break without working too hard. By stringing together five reds and five blacks, a player adds 40 points to his score. That requires just ten pots in succession. Taking the other extreme, if a player is forced to pot yellows (the colour with the smallest value) with his reds, he will need to pot fourteen reds and thirteen yellows before the break reaches 40.

With experience you will foster breakbuilding instincts. Instead of just thinking of your next shot, you will size up a situation, work out what to do and play maybe two or three shots ahead. In diagram 1 it is possible to see a six-shot sequence around the black which would help the player concerned. For someone with years of experience, the best procedure in this situation would be quite

THE MOST IMPORTANT AND MOST SATISFYING BREAK OF MY CAREER HAS TO BE THE 58 CLEARANCE TO PINK WHICH ENABLED ME TO BEAT JIMMY WHITE 18-17 IN THE FINAL OF THE 1994 EMBASSY WORLD CHAMPIONSHIP. ALTHOUGH THE BALLS WERE ALL INVITINGLY PLACED, I'VE NEVER FELT UNDER MORE PRESSURE. I TRIED TO PLAY POSITIONAL SHOTS THAT WOULD GIVE ME CHOICE. I CONCENTRATED VERY HARD ON NOT LEAVING THE CUE-BALL NEAR THE CUSHION AND, OF COURSE, I REALISED I NEEDED TO MAINTAIN RHYTHMIC, STRAIGHT CUEING.

obvious. For a novice, the unravelling of the positional puzzle might not be so straightforward.

There are millions of different positions in which the balls can come to rest, so to deal with them all would be impossible. However, there are certain principles a player should adhere to when compiling a break.

Whenever possible, try to leave yourself a choice of shots, avoid having to bridge over intervening balls to reach the cue-ball and keep the white from going into an awkward spot under or near to the cushion.

In red/black breakbuilding other more specific principles apply. Only in rare instances should a player purposely leave himself 'straight', without an angle, on the black as there is considerably less scope to manoeuvre the cue-ball. Try also to clear the paths between the black and the top pockets, should any intervening balls be causing an obstruction. A

player has a much greater margin of error if he can pot the black into both corner pockets instead of just one.

In diagram 1 a player can pot the three reds with blacks without the cue-ball touching a cushion. This is achieved by leaving an angle on the black and stunning the white into perfect position for the next red. With the reds so invitingly positioned, a whole range of options become open to a player, including the use of the cushions. In a lot of situations the cushions help a player to attain the desired position, but around the black pinpoint accuracy is needed. Diagram 1 shows the ideal circumstances for a break. On the majority of occasions you come to the table, the balls will not be so conveniently placed. Because the pack of reds is so close to the black spot, there are always unpottable and awkward reds creating positional problems. It is therefore vital to nurture the ability to control the cue-ball accurately with stun.

❶ From this ideal position for a break, a six-ball sequence around the black enables the player to pot the three reds with blacks without the cue-ball touching a cushion.

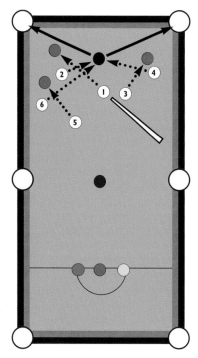

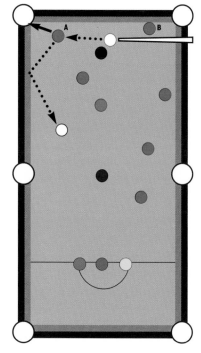

❷ At first glance, red A and red B might both appear to be obvious shots, but the better choice when breakbuilding is to pot red A and thus open up the black's path into both top pockets.

Knowing the correct choice of shot is as important for successful breakbuilding, as is good cue-ball control and a reliable technique. Diagram 2 illustrates how the correct choice of shot can enhance a breakbuilding opportunity. Red A and red B both appear to be obvious shots but, for long-term benefit, potting red A is definitely preferable. That is because when red A disappears from the table the black's path is opened up into both top pockets. This is a clear-cut example, but it does show the importance of a player being aware and alert.

BREAKBUILDING WITH OTHER COLOURS

It is undeniable that the black, because of its value, is the best colour on the table around which to construct a big break. However, as we have just seen in diagram 2, a player is often best advised to position himself on another colour (in the case of diagram 2 the blue or the pink). In addition, a player often finds

❸ When potting the red, it is possible to screw up the table with a touch of right-hand side to leave the cue-ball on the blue towards the baulk line.

that the black is awkwardly placed amongst a number of balls or tight under a cushion. In this case a sensible player accepts the limitations of the situation and chooses another colour on which to position himself. Don't become obsessed with the black, or your breakbuilding capabilities will suffer. I have seen many players attempt extremely complicated positional shots in an

'Knowing the correct choice of shot is important for successful breakbuilding.'

attempt to drop on the black when they have quite simple alternatives to get on other colours. There is no sense, or value, in this approach.

The pivotal ball in many breaks is the blue. Because of its central spot position, the blue is often more accessible than the black or pink. It is also quite frequently possible to pot the blue into any of the six pockets. In diagram 3 a player elects to screw up the table with a touch of right-hand side to leave the cue-ball on the blue towards the baulk line. If this shot is completed satisfactorily a player has two main options. He can run the cue-ball back towards the top end of the table for one of the loose reds, or elect to split the clustered pack directly behind the pink. These screw shots, from a red to blue, come up quite regularly so it is useful to practise them. Set up all angles, from full-ball through to quarter-ball. Apart from potting the red, it is crucial for the purpose of continuing the break to leave the white on the right side (the baulk side) of the blue. The screw shot from red to blue can sometimes lead to the white going perilously close to an in-off into the middle pocket (see diagram 4).

Another group of positional shots that need to be rehearsed are screw and stun shots which take the cue-ball from its position on the yellow, green or brown down towards the reds. Because of the 'remote' situation of the baulk colours, the cue-ball has to travel quite a distance, so control and touch are at a premium. The angle you have on the colour often dictates whether you have to use a cushion (as in diagram 5) which has a three-quarter-ball angle. If you are striking the object-ball full, a straightforward screw shot (diagram 6) is the most prudent choice of shot. Generally, whenever possible, it is more advantageous to play these screw shots off the yellow or green, whether or not you use a cushion. That is because the potentially expensive in-off into a middle pocket is more likely off the brown.

Screw shots are not the only option when using the baulk colours. In diagram 7, because of a combination of the slightly different position of the reds and the angle of contact required to pot the

green, a follow through shot is needed. If a player imparts the necessary topspin the cue-ball will run through, rebound off the baulk cushion and return towards the reds. This shot can be completed successfully only if enough topspin is applied. To do this, we already know that the cue-tip, running horizontally, must strike

'Another group of positional shots that need to be rehearsed are screw and stun shots.'

through the cue-ball at twelve o'clock. Any lower and stun will be unintentionally imparted, causing the cue-ball to stop well short of its intended finishing position.

One common shot using the brown can be seen clearly in diagram 8. The brown is potted into the left-hand baulk pocket and, by applying a touch of stun and right hand (running side), the cue-ball is swung around off two cushions on to the reds. The great advantage of this shot is that it leaves the cue-ball towards the middle of the playing surface. The same pot played with top and little or no sidespin would take the cue-ball towards the reds, but most likely leave it close to or under the left-hand side cushion.

So far we have assumed that there are some loose reds. Often, however, the reds are tightly clustered in a pack and need to be split in order for the break to continue. The most common way to dislodge reds from this cluster is by playing a powerful stun shot when potting the black from its spot (see diagram 9). If, for one reason or another, this particular shot is not an available option, the next best bet is to break the pack with a stun shot off the blue. The pack of reds is a big target, but some contacts on the

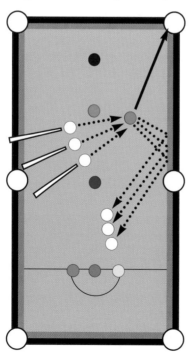

❹ The screw shot from red to blue can lead to the white going perilously close to an in-off into the middle pocket.

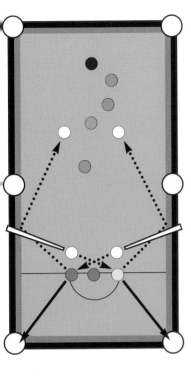

5 The angle you have on the colour often dictates whether you have to use a cushion. This shot has a three-quarter-ball angle so a cushion has to be used.

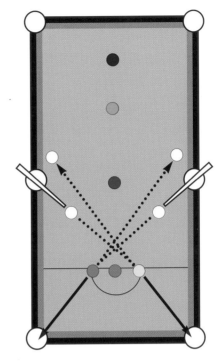

6 It is generally more advantageous to play screw shots off the yellow or green, because the potentially expensive in-off into a middle pocket is more likely off the brown.

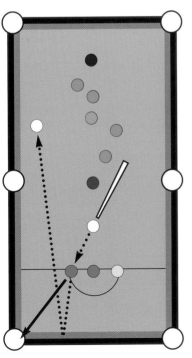

7 Because of the position of the reds and the angle of contact required to pot the green, a follow through shot is needed in this position. With enough topspin, the cue-ball will run through, rebound off the baulk cushion and return towards the reds.

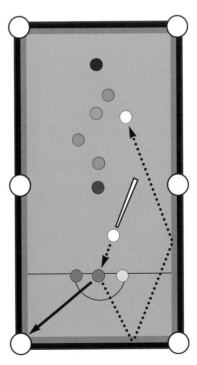

8 The brown is potted into the left-hand baulk pocket and, by applying a touch of stun and right-hand side, the cue-ball is swung around off two cushions on to the reds.

9 It is usually possible to dislodge reds from a cluster by playing a powerful stun shot when potting the black from its spot.

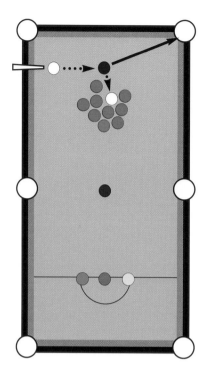

reds create more disturbance than others. If the white is sent into the pink, assuming it is on its spot at the top of the pyramid, the reds usually tend to split up favourably (as in diagram 10). On the other hand, if the cue-ball misses the pink and hits the back reds in the pack (see diagram 11) it will not split the reds as well. In addition, because it then slides off the diagonally facing pack, the cue-ball follows a path which takes it close to or into the top pocket. So it pays, for maximum effect, to take the white into the ball at the apex of the pack. James Wattana is particularly good at this type of shot.

The final splitting alternative is to take the cue-ball from either the green or yellow off the side cushion at pace into the pack. The angle exists if you leave yourself the necessary quarter to half-ball

10 If the white is sent into the pink, on its spot at the top of the pyramid, the reds usually split up favourably.

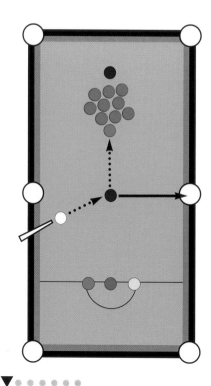

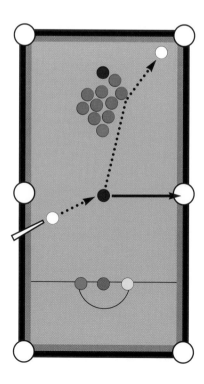

11 If the cue-ball misses the pink and hits the back reds in the pack, the position will be less favourable.

contact on the object-ball. If you do, through the correct application of running side and back spin, you will generate sufficient power to disturb the reds and, you hope, continue your break.

CHOICE OF SHOT

If, faced with a clear-cut breakbuilding opportunity, you are able to fathom out the best choice of shot from a wide range of alternatives, you are well on the road to success. Shot A and shot B may look equally beneficial to the break but, in the long run, one is preferable to the other. Treat snooker like chess. One wrong move early on in a break can lead to problems in its later stages. A classic example of how far-sighted shot selection can help in a break can be seen in diagram 12. Here, reds 1 and 2 are both easy enough to pot and position on the

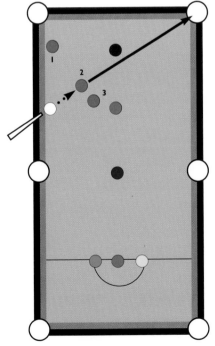

⑫ **Although at first glance, reds 1 and 2 both look easy enough to pot, it is better from this position to pot red 2, so that red 3 becomes free to be potted into either top pocket.**

black is also simple enough to attain. However, the player with an astute snooker brain will quickly realise that red 2 should be chosen as, once that is potted, red 3 becomes free to be potted into either top pocket. It is the ability to make these kind of decisions that separates a good breakbuilder from an average one.

Many players are shackled by indecision when tempted by a pot which, if missed, could present their opponent with a scoring opening. On some occasions, usually following a pinpoint safety shot, a player has no option but to attempt an extremely risky pot. This is known as a neck or nothing shot.

IN AND OUT OF BAULK OFF THE BLUE

While I would need an encyclopaedia to describe every kind of positional shot that you will come across at one time or another, one shot in particular is worth explaining in some detail. It is the one where a player is forced to take the cue-ball in and out of baulk after potting the blue to a middle pocket. If you drop on the blue at the wrong angle, it's often the only way to get back into position on the next red.

Because of the position of the baulk colours on their spots, this shot requires a player to weave the cue-ball through them. Time and again, when I first took up the game, I would unintentionally hit the yellow, green or brown with the cue-ball and lose position as a result. Gradually, I learned that this type of shot requires a deft touch, good knowledge of angles and the ability to hit the cue-ball in the right place. Of course, if one of the baulk colours is off its spot – down towards the reds, let's say – then your margin of error is much bigger.

If you look closely at professional matches, you will see a player pot the blue to a middle pocket, manoeuvre the cue-ball past the baulk colours, off the baulk cushion, back past the baulk colours and return it towards the reds. Time after time that shot helps a player recover position.

The common fault amongst average players is that they apply too much back-spin to the cue-ball, which tends to swing it towards the middle of the table and the brown. Only by trial and error, and with plenty of practice, will you learn how to play this shot well.

In most instances this shot has a better chance of positional success if you play it with running side. The cue-ball then comes off the baulk cushion at an exaggerated angle – which reduces the chances of making an unwanted contact with a baulk colour – and comes off the side cushion in such a way that it approaches the reds at a diagonal angle.

If you play the shot with check side instead, the cue-ball goes through the baulk colours and returns on a similar path after hitting the baulk cushion. You thus double the danger of hitting a baulk colour. Most players feel surer of potting the blue using check side, and you need to practise enough for this not to influence you.

The chief danger in playing with running side off the cushion (which is actually check side as it rebounds from the object-ball) is to overcut the pot. This usually happens because the cue-ball has initially been thrown off line by the side and has not returned to it by the time it strikes the blue. You can reduce this effect by making sure you get the cue well through the cue-ball rather than jabbing at it.

On the other hand, when a player has the luxury of choice about attempting a pot, he must think like an economist. He must weigh up the risk of leaving his

opponent in amongst the balls (potential loss) against the number of points likely to be scored if the pot is successful (potential profit). Obviously, if you do not consider yourself to be a good long potter, or your success ratio on a particular shot is high, you could well be forced to add other factors into account. Similarly, if it is virtually impossible to leave yourself on a colour when potting the 50/50 red, it is hardly worth the gamble. In diagram 13 a player has two possible reds 'on', even though the cue-ball is in baulk. The less experienced player might elect to pot red A with little pace on the cue-ball, in order to gain position on the black. However, although red A is nearer the pocket than red B, it is a far more dangerous shot. The smallest cueing error, or even the table rolling off, can cause the pot to go astray. Shot B is the one to choose even though it is a more difficult pot. The wise old head would attempt to pot red

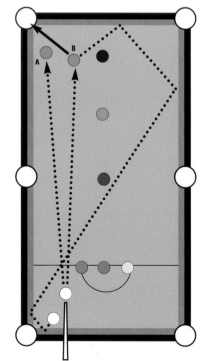

13 Although red A is nearer the pocket, it is a far more dangerous shot. It's better to attempt to pot red B with enough pace to ensure that if it is missed, the cue-ball will return to safety in the region of baulk.

B with enough pace to ensure that if it was missed the cue-ball would return to safety in the region of baulk. This is called a shot to nothing – a type of shot I will be discussing at greater length in the section on tactics.

Another common mistake made by inexperienced players is attempting to split the pack of reds at the earliest conceivable opportunity. Next time you watch a professional play, notice that, in most instances, he will clear the loose reds before thinking about splitting the pack with two or three left. This, of course, does not always hold true. If, for example, a player has the perfect angle for a split and a red is hanging over a pocket, easily pottable no matter where the cue-ball finishes, he will not pass up the chance of dislodging some reds from the cluster. However, in many instances it is wise to bide your time.

'Never hurry into the choice of shot if you are unsure.'

It is better to make 30 points from the reds already loose than to make eight and find yourself unable to continue the break. Always bear in mind that at whatever standard you play, splitting the pack is a gamble. Sometimes the reds obligingly split ideally for a player to go on and make a sizeable break. Then there are the frustrating occasions when, even though the cue-ball has been hit with force, few reds are dislodged and the break comes to an end.

Although you should guard against indecisiveness, never hurry into the choice of shot if you are unsure. It can be fatal to rush in and impetuously play the first shot that comes into your head. Without being too ponderous, you must weigh up the alternatives available and act accordingly. It is also important to concentrate your full attention on the shot when you are playing it. Blank everything else out when down on the shot; it's no time to start wondering whether or not you have made the correct shot selection. If you are in two minds and your concentration is not 100 per cent, it is a fair bet that the shot will go astray.

Even at top professional level, this is sometimes easier said than done. How many times do you see a player potting every ball you would expect to see a player of his standard pot, only for him to fail at one which is no more difficult in itself but which represents the key to a frame?

There is a plausible scientific explanation for this. The brain's alpha waves control physical performance, co-ordination if you like, and the beta waves control thinking. It is when the beta waves cut across the alpha in the course of actually playing the shot – by allowing the mind to linger on the significance of the shot or, in the worst cases, by assuming that victory is a formality and letting the mind race ahead – that the shot is very likely to be missed.

If you can treat the shot simply on its merits and just concentrate on playing it as well as you can, then the alpha patterns of the brain won't be interfered with.

I never worked this out scientifically for myself, but just knew instinctively that the more I could concentrate on the shot just as a shot, the better it would be. One of the benefits of good positional play is that you can play from shot to shot without having to think very much. If you keep losing position, though, and have to do a lot of thinking for every shot, concentration has to be built up for each shot after you have taken time out for thinking.

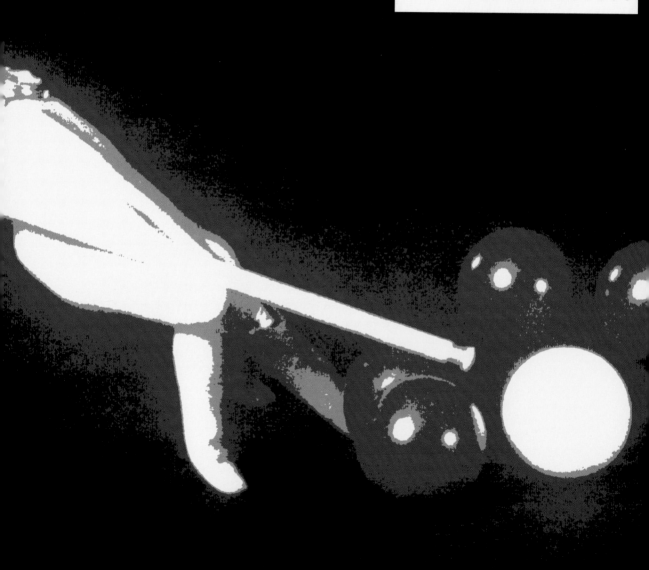

8

ADVANCED
SHOTS

There are instances in which a conventional pot is not possible and a player has no option but to play safe. However, on other occasions, spectacular but very makeable shots present themselves and a scoring sequence can be launched or continued as a result. While these groups of advanced shots are not immediately obvious to the novice, the more experienced player is always on the lookout for them. Doubles, sets and plants have often proved to be a turning point in important matches, and anyone who can consistently complete them successfully has a distinct advantage over someone who cannot.

DOUBLES

The double is a stroke employed quite regularly by professionals and players of a high standard. Yet many other players ignore it or, on the rare occasions when they choose to play it, their approach is far from confident. Although the double has a small margin of error, it is a very useful shot to have at your disposal.

A double means striking the object-ball into one or more cushions at such an angle that it rebounds into a pocket. Doubles are usually played into middle pockets, although sometimes they are attempted into the corners. Assuming your alignment, sighting and cue delivery are sufficiently effective to allow you to hit the object-ball where you want, the success rate of this shot depends entirely on your knowledge of the angle of rebound from a cushion. This varies from table to table and also on the pace at which the object-ball is struck on to the cushion. The harder the object-ball is struck, the more difficult it becomes to make an accurate judgement of the angle of rebound.

It is true to say that a ball struck with firm but not extreme strength will rebound off a cushion at precisely the reverse angle to that at which it hit. The path of the object-ball can therefore be mapped out as a V, a fact that should be the basis for your sighting of all conventional doubles. As with all forms of potting, your ability to play an accurate double will improve with your knowledge of angles.

The most commonly played type of double is the one shown in diagram 1. Here, the object-ball is close to the side cushion and the angle of rebound required to send it into the opposite middle pocket is relatively simple to compute.

In diagram 2 the object-ball is much further away from the middle pocket (its intended target) and the angle at which

'The experienced player is always on the lookout for the spectacular but very makeable shots which sometimes present themselves.'

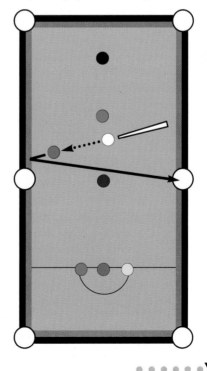

❶ DOUBLE
This is the most commonly played type of double. With the object-ball close to the side cushion, it is fairly easy to compute the angle of rebound required to send the object-ball into the opposite middle pocket.

These three photographs show how I go about completing a routine double on the blue to a middle pocket. You can see that the blue's path to and from the cushion is V-shaped.

it must leave the cushion is also less straightforward. In this shot a player must select the right angle of rebound, as well as fathoming out the correct initial contact between cue-ball and object-ball. On paper this might not appear too difficult. In reality this shot, and others similar to it, are fraught with danger. It is therefore usually wise, whenever possible, to turn down a double unless there is a strong likelihood that the cue-ball can be manoeuvred into a safe position. Diagram 3 shows two regular cut back doubles, which allow a player to take them on happy in the knowledge that he can get the ball back to safety.

In the majority of cases, doubles into

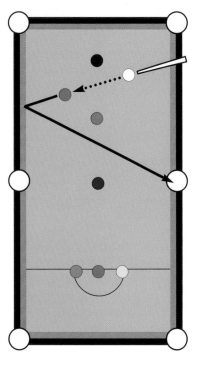

2 *DOUBLE*
This is a more complicated situation than that in diagram 1, requiring exactly the right angle of rebound as well as initial contact between cue-ball and object-ball.

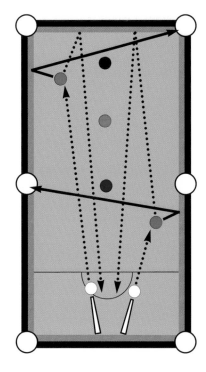

3 *CUT BACK DOUBLE*
A player can take on these two regular cut back doubles, confident that the ball can be returned to safety. More often than not, doubles into corner pockets are far riskier than those into middle pockets.

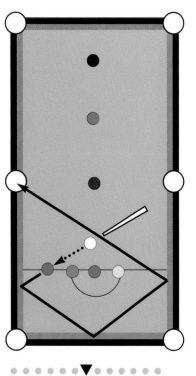

4 *COCKED HAT DOUBLE*
A three cushion shot into a middle pocket is generally safer than a double into a corner pocket. The cocked hat double is so called because of its symmetry and shape.

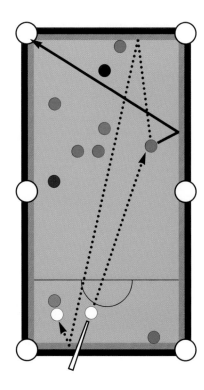

5 *CROSS DOUBLE*
This is a risky shot, but if you can pull it off the cue-ball returns to safety. Making the simpler pot into the top right-hand pocket in this situation would make safety much harder to achieve.

corner pockets represent a far greater risk than those into middle pockets. So hazardous are they that it is impossible to recommend them. The alternative, in some instances, to a corner pocket double is a three cushion shot (see diagram 4) into the more open middle pocket. This so-called cocked hat double once won me a very big frame on the black. Like the range of cross doubles, it can often be combined with safety.

In diagram 5 a player who can recognise the right choice of shot will play the cross double into the top left-hand pocket. By applying a touch of left-hand side to the cue-ball, he is able to bring it back down the table into baulk, off the bottom cushion and in behind the green for an awkward snooker. If the double is successful, it is possible to pot the brown and position the cue-ball back on the reds. If the double does go astray, the snooker acts as your insurance policy. Doubles are shots for the opportunist. Be aware of the advantage you can gain from them and don't be afraid to play them if the situation warrants.

SETS AND PLANTS

Sets and plants, like doubles, can turn a frame. They can present themselves at any stage of a frame, but are most common early on when the reds are close together, packed between the pink and black spot. A set arises when two object-balls, usually reds, are touching in such a way that contact between the first and the cue-ball sends the second into the pocket. The pot is completed if the cue-ball strikes the first object-ball at virtually any angle (see diagram 6). Only a thin contact, which causes a squeeze effect, can lead to the second object-ball missing its intended target, the pocket.

Because the margin of error is so great on this shot, the key is to be able to identify a set amongst such a cluster of balls. Spotting sets is often the most crucial aspect of the shot.

When you are left with a pot, you should always attempt to gain position after potting it. The same principle applies with a set. However, because a wide range of contacts allows the ball to be potted, a player's positional possibilities are extensive off a set. Two important points must be remembered when playing position from a set. If you are playing with topspin, you will need to apply more of it than normal to attain the necessary follow through required. Conversely, if you are screwing back, less backspin than normal needs to be

> ### 'Doubles into corner pockets are so hazardous that it is impossible to recommend them'

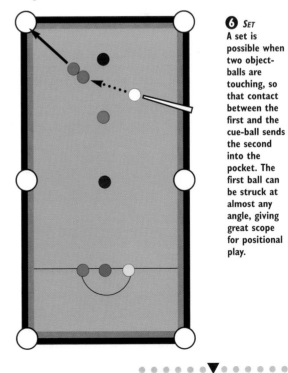

6 SET
A set is possible when two object-balls are touching, so that contact between the first and the cue-ball sends the second into the pocket. The first ball can be struck at almost any angle, giving great scope for positional play.

In this instance the two reds are close together and 'set on' for the pocket.

'As with so many other aspects of snooker, practice and practical experience need to be banked in large quantities.'

when a 'rogue' cue-ball, of slightly smaller size or less weight than the object-balls, is wrongly used.)

Diagram 7 illustrates the difference between a plant and a set. A plant goes wrong more often because the two object-balls, rather than touching, have a distance between them. As a result, the first object-ball has to make contact with the second object-ball at the correct angle to complete the pot successfully. With a conventional pot, a player has only to fathom the angle of contact needed between cue-ball and object-ball. With a plant, a third factor is added to the increasingly compli-cated calculation, for a player has to work out not only this contact but also the contact needed between the first and second object-balls.

imparted. This is because the cue-ball is, in essence, making contact with a body twice as heavy as an ordinary object-ball. Therefore the resistance offered is twice as great as with one red. The result of this is that screw shots come back further with considerably less spin. (The same applies under normal circumstances

The best way to compute both con-tact angles is to imagine a point on the distant cushion at which to aim the first object-ball. If your alignment is correct, its path to the cushion will be blocked by the second object-ball and contact between them will send the second object-ball into the pocket.

Generally speaking, the greater the distance between the object-balls, the greater the risk of failure. Three and four-ball plants are sometimes attempted, but these carry a large degree of risk and should be taken on only if it is easy to run the cue-ball into a safe position. The difficulty in gauging these shots is such that it takes a considerable learning period before a player develops a reasonably high success rate with them. As with so many other aspects of snooker previously discussed in this book, practice and practical experience need to be banked in large quantities before a player can rely on himself as a good player of plants.

Of the players currently competing on

The bigger the distance between the two reds, the more weighing up the shot requires and the more risk of missing it.

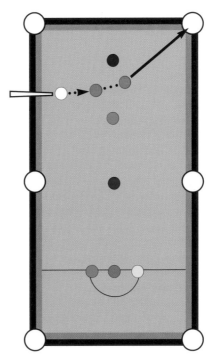

7 PLANT
A set simply has to be correctly spotted. A plant requires the calculation of two angles because you are playing two object-balls with distance between them. As a rule, the greater the distance between the object-balls, the more difficult it is to play a successful plant.

the professional circuit, I think Cliff Thorburn and Alain Robidoux – both Canadians – are the best at plants that I have come across. Both come from a similar playing background – an environment where they also played American pool, usually for money. I am not, of course, suggesting this is the only way to become a competent player of plants. At the end of a practice session, or a few frames, fill up any spare minutes by experimenting with certain plants. After a while you will begin to develop an improved feel for this type of shot. Plants are not only spectacular, they are often the key that unlocks a frame-winning break.

POTTING BALLS ALONG A CUSHION

Screw shots, swerves and plants are particularly troublesome shots for a large percentage of the world's snooker-playing population; as is potting balls

DRAG

BACKSPIN IS USED NOT ONLY FOR SCREW AND STUN SHOTS BUT ALSO WHEN APPLYING THE EFFECT KNOWN AS DRAG. THE DRAG SHOT, USED FREQUENTLY BY PLAYERS OF AN ADVANCED STANDARD, IS DESIGNED TO ALLOW THE CUE-BALL TO BE STRUCK RELATIVELY FIRMLY, BUT ALSO SLOWLY, OVER A REASONABLE DISTANCE.

IF THE CUE-BALL IS IN THE REGION OF BAULK AND A RED IS INVITINGLY PLACED OVER A TOP POCKET SOME TEN TO TWELVE FEET AWAY, A PLAYER HAS TWO POSITIONAL CHOICES IF HE WANTS TO LEAVE HIMSELF ON THE BLACK (WHICH IS ON ITS SPOT) FOR THE NEXT SHOT. HE CAN SIMPLY ROLL THE WHITE DOWN THE TABLE, BUT IN SO DOING IS VULNERABLE TO THE TABLE ROLLING OFF AND CAUSING THE CUE-BALL TO DEVIATE FROM ITS INTENDED COURSE.

THE ALTERNATIVE IS THE DRAG SHOT. TO APPLY DRAG, STRIKE THE CUE-BALL, AS YOU WOULD FOR A SCREW SHOT, BELOW CENTRE TOWARDS SIX O'CLOCK. INITIALLY THE BACKSPIN IMPARTED WILL HOLD UP THE BALL AND IT IS THUS POSSIBLE TO STRIKE THE CUE-BALL MUCH HARDER THAN YOU WOULD HAVE TO FOR THE ROLL SHOT. EVENTUALLY, BECAUSE THE CUE-BALL IS TRAVELLING A LONG WAY OVER THE SURFACE OF THE TABLE, THE BACKSPIN WILL DISSIPATE AND BEFORE MAKING CONTACT WITH THE OBJECT-BALL IT WILL BEGIN A FORWARD ROTATION. APART FROM ADDING A PRECISE EDGE TO A PLAYER'S POSITIONAL SKILLS, THE DRAG SHOT OFTEN ALLOWS A TABLE'S IDIOSYNCRATIC ROLL OFFS TO BE CONQUERED.

top cushion. The nap, running from baulk to the top end of a table, pulls a ball into the top cushion but away from the baulk cushion. To counteract this tendency, the pot can be struck with greater pace, although this in itself can be counter-productive as the heavier the shot the greater the likelihood of the object-ball wriggling in the pocket's jaws. As with all advanced shots, potting along a cushion can be mastered only by practice and experimentation. Often with these shots it is incorrect sighting, as opposed to crooked cue delivery, which causes problems. Ultimately the decision whether or not to attempt a pot along the cushion is down to the individual concerned. You may err on the side of caution and try to pot another less difficult shot or play safe. So be it. However, if you elect to take on a cushion pot, always be positive. Go for it 100 per cent and harness your concentration on the shot accordingly.

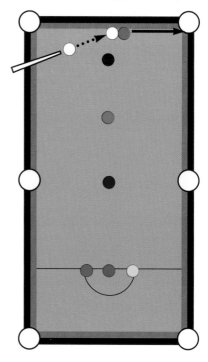

8 *CUSHION POT* In order to pot the red from this situation, the cue-ball must make simultaneous contact with it and the top cushion. If either the cushion or the red is struck first, the shot will miss its target.

along a cushion. Yet while it would be foolish to suggest that these shots are easy, it is also wrong to ignore them completely owing to a fear of failure.

The most common cushion pots are seen at the top/black end of the table. In diagram 8, for the red to be potted the cue-ball has to make simultaneous contact with it and the top cushion. If the cushion is struck first, or the red, the shot will stray from its intended target. Because of the pulling effect of the nap, it is generally easier to pot balls along the

WEARING SPECTACLES

● The ability to sight your shots accurately is imperative if you are to compete at a high level, for snooker is a game where a fraction of an inch either way can often spell the difference between failure and success. It is a fact of life that some people's eyesight is better than others; and for those with eyesight deficiencies, however small, visual aids are required. Luckily, I have perfect eyesight but John Pulman and Fred Davis wore glasses to win their world titles, as did Dennis Taylor (right) in 1985. Dennis's story is one that proves that a player's game can undergo a dramatic change for the better if he decides to employ glasses to overcome any sighting and alignment difficulties. Dennis had worn glasses for reading since his youth but it was not until 1979, aged 30, that he began to experiment with contact lenses. After two frustrating years of perseverance, Dennis ditched them in favour of the pair of swivel lens glasses that were to revolutionise his career.

For these spectacles Dennis went to Jack Karnehm, a former snooker commentator on the BBC who had been trained by his father, an oculist, to make spectacle frames. Dennis freely admits now that there was more than one occasion during this initial breaking-in period when he could easily have thrown them away. No doubt many amateurs will experience similar teething problems when attempting to adapt to glasses. However, these 'upside down' spectacles, which are designed to prevent their rims getting in the way of a player as he sights the shots, are well worth getting used to. Dennis eventually began to reap the benefits, especially on long-range shots.

The oversized glasses became his hallmark and, when we visited Guangzhou in October 1990 for the Asian Open, they were one of the factors that made him an instant hit with the Chinese public. I won the tournament but Dennis, with those glasses and his trick shots, stole the show. The point of this tale is to impress on all players the importance of recognising difficulties with sighting and acting on them accordingly.

Glasses, contact lenses or whatever are not guaranteed to cure all the ills in the game for a player with defective eyesight. However, ocular help can only be of benefit in the long run. Players afflicted by short-sightedness require the sort of lenses that sharpen up blurred images at distance without having an adverse effect on the image of balls close to the player. If near vision is impaired by inappropriate lenses, such as it would be with ordinary reading glasses, the use of a visual aid would be extremely counter-productive on close-range shots.

Obviously the specially designed bifocal glasses needed for snooker are not cheap but, while they can be a handicap

initially, they can develop into the key that allows a player to reach his full potential. If your sighting difficulties are relatively minor, the cost of glasses, the thought of the breaking-in period, and the glare from the balls one can sometimes get would be enough to put you off the idea – and rightly so. On the other hand, if a player's eyesight makes it impossible to sight long-range shots accurately, spectacles or contact lenses are strongly recommended. Most players first take up the game with excellent eyesight which slowly deteriorates with the passage of time.

A surprisingly large number of players refuse to accept they have a problem and, as a result, their overall performance steadily crumbles and their confidence is gradually eroded. I just hope, if and when the time arrives, that I am sensible enough to take corrective action. The wearing of spectacles is not ideal but if your eyesight worsens, they can be a very welcome lifeline.

Fred Davis, one of the game's all-time greats, suffered from myopia when he was my age, but was too self-conscious to tell anyone. However, he was stung into action by his humiliating 17-14 defeat by W. A. Withers in the first round of the 1937 World Championship. With his career and future uncertain, he took the decision to consult an optician. He was issued with the first set of swivel lens spectacles, which he could tilt so that he was looking squarely through the lens when he was down on the shot. From 1948 to 1956 he reigned supreme, winning the world title eight times in nine years.

While everyone gains pleasure from potting balls, building a break and attaining an excellent position, these aspects of the game are not, in isolation, sufficient for a player to reach a high standard. Safety play is a vital weapon in any player's armoury, for without it, skills such as potting and position cannot be regularly displayed.

If your tactical play is defective and you fail to place your opponent in an awkward position on a regular basis, his mistakes will be limited. In turn, your scoring chances will be restricted and you will find it difficult to win frames easily. Safety, like money, is a means to an end, rather than an end in itself.

BREAKING OFF

Often, because the break-off shot starts a frame, players do not treat it with the concentration it deserves, yet a careless break-off shot can often set the tone for a frame. Obviously, the higher the standard at which one is playing, the more influential the break-off. On a number of occasions during my professional career I've made a complete hash of the break-off shot and been forced to sit out an 80-plus, frame-winning break.

Many novices, under the misguided impression that any old safety shot is sufficient for the break-off, roll the cue-ball down the table gently into the pack of reds causing the minimum of displacement. Fair enough, this ensures safety but it immediately hands the initiative to your opponent. Instead of a positive safety break-off, which leaves him in an awkward spot from which he is likely to commit an error, he can easily glance off the pack of reds and run to safety. With the correct approach, it is possible to place your opponent in trouble, so never pass up the chance to break-off if you win the toss.

Professionals use a number of different breaks to gain the upper hand, all of which involve the use of side, leave the balls safe and ensure that the white returns safely behind the baulk line, leaving the opponent with a difficult opening shot. Too intricate and skilful a break should be avoided by the beginner as, played inaccurately, it can prove expensive. Diagram 1 shows an uncomplicated break-off which does not include the use of side. By hitting the cue-ball centrally, glancing the reds and coming off the top and side cushion, you can return the white safely to baulk. A quarter-ball contact on the outside red is required if this shot is to be successful.

> 'Safety play is a vital weapon in any player's armoury. Without it you can't display your other skills'

❶ This uncomplicated break-off does not include the use of side. By hitting the cue-ball centrally, glancing the reds with a quarter-ball contact on the outside red, and coming off the top and side cushion, the white can be returned safely to baulk.

By imparting running side (in the case of diagram 2 right-hand side), you can hit the same red, but the cue-ball will swing to the opposite side of the blue from diagram 1 on its return to the bottom cushion. To apply this sidespin, it is necessary to strike the cue-ball between three and four o'clock. The advantage of this particular break is that it leads to a greater movement of the reds than the 'novice' break shown in diagram 1. Most professionals choose to use this kind of advanced break as, by splitting the pack, it is more likely that your opponent will leave you a clear-cut breakbuilding chance should he make a mistake.

Many top-quality players tend to risk a more complicated break-off which, if successful, pays greater dividends. Move the white across the baulk line towards the yellow, apply even more side and, crucially, hit the second or even third red from the pack's edge (see diagram 3). This is a break often used by the game's more attacking players such as Jimmy White and Tony Drago. By applying so much spin, the reds often open invitingly, the cue-ball returns to baulk and the opponent is immediately faced with a difficult situation. However, as in many other snooker positions, shots that pay rich dividends tend to carry a high degree of risk should they go wrong. Often, if the contact on the red aimed for is slightly too thin, the cue-ball will make a secondary contact with the next red down the pack and will slide towards a possible in-off into the right-hand top pocket. Even if it does not go into the pocket, there is a strong likelihood that the cue-ball will catch the jaws of the pocket and fail to return to baulk.

> *'A good break-off can give you an important early advantage, while a bad one can easily lead to your defeat in that frame.'*

❷ By imparting running side, it is possible to hit the same red as in diagram I, but in this instance the cue-ball will swing to the opposite side of the blue on its return to the bottom cushion.

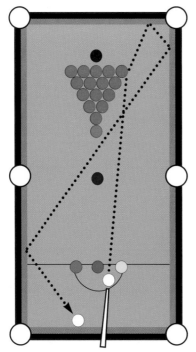

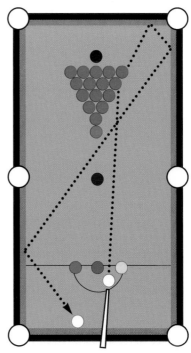

❸ Top-quality players can risk a more complicated break-off, by moving the white across the baulk line towards the yellow, applying more side and hitting the second or even third red from the pack's edge.

Should the reds be caught too thick, there will be a similar outcome.

Even if the wrong type of contact on the reds is avoided, there is then the lesser, but nevertheless very real, problem of making an unwanted contact on the blue as the cue-ball returns to baulk and safety. As Frank Callan is inclined to say: whatever you do don't hit the blue.

Why not practise a break-off shot should you encounter problems with them? Remember: a good break-off can give you an important early advantage, while a bad one can easily lead to your defeat in that frame.

SAFETY PLAY

It is obvious that safety play on its own cannot win frames and consequently matches, but it is also true that a lack of tactical expertise will be a very serious deficiency. If you have difficulty in creating openings for yourself, your scoring power will be seriously compromised, rather like a soccer team that is let down by an ineffective midfield. At amateur level it is sometimes possible to see a frame of snooker become an extension of the story of the tortoise and the hare. A good potter comes up against a wily tactician who keeps him tight, forces a string of errors and, from the resultant leaves, accrues sufficient points to win the frame, usually to the utter exasperation of an opponent who knows he is the better potter and therefore assumes he is a better player.

At an early stage of your snooker development, safety play may not appear that important as, most likely, you will be playing someone who cannot take advantage of a gilt-edged breakbuilding opportunity should you present him with one. Do not be fooled. As your game improves and you compete against better, more experienced opponents, the

true value of safety play will reveal itself. There are no hard and fast rules concerning the right and wrong time to play safe. In the same situation, even at professional level, two players may elect to take on two completely different shots, but usually experience – or a lack of this most valuable snooker asset – will be the key to your choice of shot in a particular situation.

When a player stands over a shot which affords him more than one option, there are a number of influential factors he must try to balance against each other before choosing which course of action to follow. These include the condition of the table, the score of both the match and the frame, how many balls remain on the table, the standard of the opposition and, perhaps most important of all, how the player concerned views the particular shot. If, for instance, he has played poorly in the match to that point and is short of confidence, it is likely that a 50/50 pot will be refused in favour of safety. On the other hand, if a player is potting well, has made a number of sizeable breaks and holds a useful lead in the match, he is more likely to take on the same 50/50 pot because his confidence is high. Weighing the pros and cons correctly is vital in such a position. Dennis Taylor, still one of the hardest match players on the professional circuit, likens this 'do I, don't I?' decision to the kind of quandary a businessman finds himself in. Basically, Taylor wisely believes that, unless no other option is available, it is

> I MUST ADMIT THAT ONE OF MY FAULTS OVER THE YEARS HAS BEEN A TENDENCY TO GO FOR THE ODD 'LUNATIC' SHOT AS IAN DOYLE, MY MANAGER, CALLS THEM. SOME PLAYERS TEND TO BECOME NEGATIVE UNDER PRESSURE, BUT I'M CERTAINLY NOT ONE OF THEM. NO PLAYER CHOOSES THE RIGHT SHOT ALL THE TIME, ALTHOUGH STEVE DAVIS AND MY COUNTRYMAN, ALAN MCMANUS, COME PRETTY CLOSE.

foolish to take a significant risk for an insignificant profit. Playing with a big risk for a big gain can also be foolish, says Taylor, and I would tend, on the whole, to agree with him. Of course, it is all a question of being clever enough to play the percentages in such a way that, for the most part, they are stacked in your favour. Therefore a sensible player, whenever possible, will seek the shot that gives a big gain for a small risk.

> *'Whenever possible, a sensible player will play the percentages, seeking the shot that gives a big gain for a small risk.'*

While you must always guard against becoming too negative and safety-orientated, it is important to remember that good safety not only increases the likelihood of your opponent making mistakes but also tends to make him become frustrated, out of touch when it comes to compiling a break and less confident. Conversely, if you find yourself a victim of someone's safety expertise, it is vital to bide your time. Be patient, composed and never try to force the situation by taking on a pot you know you should not be going for. Be patient, take pride in replying with even better safety and, in terms of winning a higher proportion of frames, you will benefit.

SHOT TO NOTHING

Working on the principle that any shot with a big gain for a small risk is desirable, the attentive, tactically alert player who is able to spot a shot to nothing is at an advantage. I explained this type of shot when discussing doubles, sets and plants, but I'll define it again as one where you can take on a pot, miss and still leave your opponent without a scoring opportunity.

A classic example of a shot to nothing is shown in diagram 4. The player can attempt to pot the red into the top left-hand pocket, knowing full well that the cue-ball has an unimpeded, natural path back to baulk. If the red wobbles in the jaws of the pocket it could be left, but with the other reds so widely spread it is likely they will block a clear path to it. If the red is potted and the cue-ball comes to rest in the position shown in diagram 4, it will be easy to pot the brown into the middle pocket, take the cue-ball back down towards the pack of reds and possibly launch a sizeable break. If, however, the cue-ball stops in position 2 and an obvious pot is not readily available, the player can quietly roll up to either the yellow or the brown, thereby leaving his opponent in an extremely dangerous snooker. When you have sufficient cue-ball control it is possible to execute the deep screw to nothing shot, shown in diagram 5.

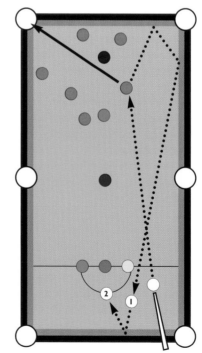

4 In this classic example of a shot to nothing, the player can attempt to pot the red into the top left-hand pocket, knowing that the cue-ball has an unimpeded, natural path back to baulk.

On old television clips I have seen Bill Werbeniuk produce some incredible shots of this nature. Not everyone possesses such cue power but, even for those with less power, the screw back shot to nothing is still possible on many occasions, especially when the red with which you aim to make the initial contact is relatively close to the baulk region.

> *'These shots do not frequently present themselves, but when they do it pays to take full advantage.'*

The final point to bear in mind with a shot to nothing is that maximum concentration should always be applied to completing the pot successfully. Just think, here you have the chance possibly to launch a big break without any risk. Don't be negative and think half-heartedly that it doesn't really matter what happens to the pot as you'll be safe

anyway. That's like someone being handed a free ticket for a lottery and saying, 'I don't mind whether I win or not, it hasn't cost me anything.' These shots do not frequently present themselves, but when they do it pays to take advantage.

POSITIVE SAFETY

This advice to think positively holds true in all forms of tactical play. When possible, be positive with a safety shot. Not only should you attempt to leave the balls in a safe position, you should carefully work out where you can play the cue-ball to make it the most awkward for your opponent. If you negatively play safe, the chances are that he will put you in trouble and thus seize the initiative which you should have held.

Assuming a frame involves two tactically capable, experienced players, the opening exchanges will usually be predominantly safety orientated. Even if you've seen snooker only on television, you could hardly have failed to notice that this usually involves making a series of thin contacts with reds situated in the top third of the table to bring the cue-ball back to the safety of baulk. Although at first glance it may appear that the players are merely going through the motions, waiting for an opening to present itself, this is not the case at top level. They are working out where to put the cue-ball to make life as difficult as possible for the next player to the table. Sometimes the pace of the game slows to a crawl as these master tacticians weigh up all the options in a bid to outwit each other.

One of the most important factors in a successful break-off is a significant dislodging of the reds from the pack. The same applies with many safety shots in the early stages of a frame. Remember that if you are confident enough to move

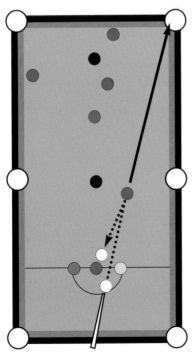

5 With sufficient cue-ball control, it is possible to execute this deep screw to nothing shot.

the reds into more easily pottable positions when playing safe, your chances of making a break, should your opponent make a mistake, will increase dramatically. Knowing this, the pressure on your opponent to fashion an adequate reply will also increase, as will his likelihood to fail. While this shot has its clear advantages it also has the accompanying pitfalls. With the balls so widely spread they provide additional obstacles to the cue-ball on its path back to baulk. It is wise to take on these shots only when you

> **'Even the very best players sometimes abandon logic in favour of personal judgement.'**

are certain, or as certain as you can be, that you can get safe. Positive safety play is fine but don't go overboard.

There is often a dilemma facing all players, at all levels, when it comes to choosing between attack or defence, safety or pot. The choice is down to the player at the table, no one else, and many overlapping factors have a direct effect on the decision.

In diagram 6 a common problem presents itself. When faced with position A, should the player err on the side of caution and trickle the cue-ball behind the yellow or brown, or should he elect to pot the tricky yellow into the left-hand middle pocket? The position of the reds should be the most influential factor in the decision. Bearing in mind that potting the yellow is anything but a formality, it would be sensible to lay the snooker if the reds were well spread. However, if the reds are packed tightly together, there is no harm in going for the yellow. This is for two very good reasons. Firstly, if you lay a snooker with the reds clustered together, the target area for a successful escape is large and,

even if your opponent misses, it will not cause too much damage. Secondly, when there is a chance of accruing two points (by potting the yellow) with very little risk attached, it should not usually be passed up.

Basically, the attack/defence balance is swayed by the difficulty of the pot. If, rather than being tricky, the brown is a straightforward pot into the middle pocket (as in position B diagram 6), my advice is to take the bull by the horns and take it on. In these kind of instances, the player's thoughts should not be centred on what would happen should he miss, but on making a frame-winning break from the opening.

All this assumes that players tend to apply logic to problematical situations. Some do, but most, even the very best, sometimes abandon logic in favour of personal judgement. Some players fancy a particular shot which others may dread. Another influential factor to bear

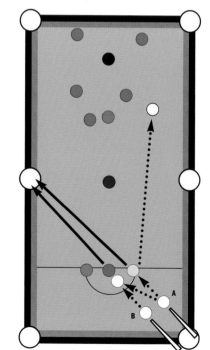

6 From position A, it is probably better to lay a snooker, rather than attempting to pot the yellow. If, as in position B, the brown is a straight-forward pot into the middle pocket, it is wisest to take it on.

in mind is the score at the time of the shot. For instance, if a player is well behind, he may feel unable to take on a pot he would not hesitate to try if he held a healthy lead. This is clearly shown in diagram 7 with a straightforward pot on the last red into the bottom right-hand pocket. If player A was 34 points ahead, he would cheerfully pot the red, leaving his opponent 35 behind and requiring two snookers to tie with just the six colours remaining.

However, player B, because he is 34 points behind with only one red remaining, would be extremely foolish to do anything other than refuse the pot in favour of safety. The red may be easy enough but, with the pink and black tied up in unpottable positions on the opposite side cushion, it would be virtually impossible to score the six or seven points off a colour needed to avoid being at the snookers required stage. Player B could pot the red and screw down for

❼ When selecting a shot, it is advisable to bear in mind the score. If you are ahead and confident when faced with this position, you should pot the red, but if you are behind, it's wiser to go for safety and refuse the pot.

the blue from its spot, but the six points gained, plus the 27 available for the colours, add up to 33 – one short of the 34 needed to force a respotted black.

An extension of this type of thinking is involved with other types of safety shots. If a player is behind, he will be more inclined to try safety shots that allow him to knock awkwardly placed colours into the open so that his chances of a recovery improve. Conversely, it is common at an advanced level to see a player with a substantial lead deliberately put one of the colours out of commission, usually tight under a cushion or against another ball. By doing this, the player gives himself a degree of insurance against his opponent wiping away his arrears in one go with a frame-winning clearance.

'It is common at an advanced level to see a player with a substantial lead deliberately put one of the colours out of commission.'

Time and again in Spencers Snooker Club in Stirling, I have watched as a novice ties himself in knots with what he believes to be the correct choice of shot. One of the most frequently recurring faults with these inexperienced players is to attempt a pot and safety off a colour. In diagram 8 a player pots the blue into a distant baulk pocket and runs the cue-ball to safety under the bottom cushion. If the pot is missed there's no problem. However, if it's successful, the player concerned will suddenly find himself facing a potentially dangerous safety shot. Should he make an error and leave his opponent in amongst the reds, the five points accrued from potting the blue will be of little comfort. If you feel confident of potting the blue, it is much more advisable to stun over into the

8 If from this position you successfully pot the blue into a distant baulk pocket and run the cue-ball to safety under the bottom cushion, you will find yourself facing a potentially dangerous shot.

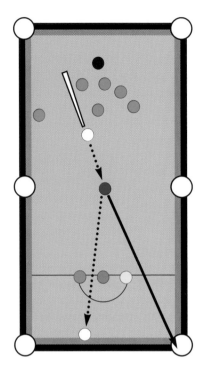

9 If you feel confident of potting the blue, it is advisable to stun over into the middle table, leaving yourself a simple return to baulk with the next shot.

middle of the table (see diagram 9) to leave yourself a simple enough return to baulk with your next shot.

When playing safe, always be aware of the dangers of a double kiss and be able to spot the kind of situation where one is likely to occur. A double kiss occurs when the cue-ball and object-ball make a second, unwanted contact which, in many instances, prevents the cue-ball returning to a safe position. Obviously, if you think the likelihood of a double kiss is high, it pays to seek an alternative route to safety.

SNOOKERING

Earlier in this chapter, I stated that safety play was a means to an end rather than an end in itself, and this also applies to snookering your opponent. Apart from at the tail end of a frame, when you need the penalty points from a missed snooker to be able to win, snookers themselves are not primarily laid as a

means of accruing points. Their main function is to force your rival into committing an error which directly leads to a scoring opportunity.

A lot of club players take great pleasure in snookering their opponent time and again to show they can stop him scoring. This is all very well if there is no simple scoring shot available. If, however, a player chooses to play a snooker in preference to a pot that could directly lead to a frame-winning opening, he is his own worst enemy.

On the other hand, do not become one of those players who contemplate laying snookers only when they need the points at the end of a frame. An awkward snooker can be an invaluable

'An awkward snooker can be an invaluable weapon at any time during a frame, or indeed a match.'

10 Here, the player who has to attempt an escape from the snooker behind the yellow is in deep trouble, for not only is it difficult to hit the object-balls, but it is virtually impossible to leave the cue-ball in a safe position.

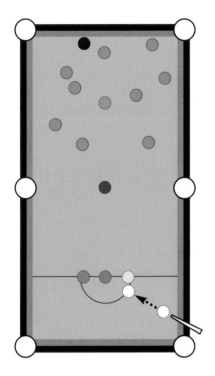

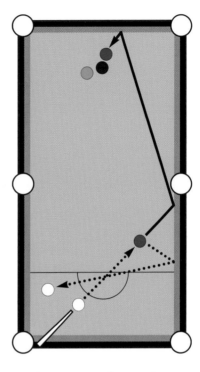

11 A snooker has been laid with only the blue, pink and black on the table. The blue has been doubled off the right-hand side cushion behind the pink and black, which are close together at the top end of the table.

weapon at any time during a frame, or indeed a match. In diagram 10 the player who has to attempt an escape from the snooker behind the yellow is in deep trouble. Not only is it difficult to hit the object-balls, but it is virtually impossible to leave the cue-ball in a safe position.

Only with experience and a steadily gained knowledge of tactics will you increase your percentage of correct shot selections when it comes to snookers. However, I can point out a number of guidelines which even the novice is advised to take on board.

When you try to lay a snooker, your first objective, rather than the snooker itself, should be to leave the object-ball safe as an insurance against the snooker not being obtained. On this basis, it follows that an attempted snooker in which the object-ball is struck towards a pocket should be played only if it is easy or if there is no alternative.

When you need a snooker in order to

win a frame, your chances decrease as the number of balls remaining on the table decreases. From this some players misguidedly believe that, if their opponents need snookers, they should roll balls over pockets. But if they do, an opponent can pot the ball deliberately left and manoeuvre the cue-ball into a favourable position from which to lay a successful snooker on the next colour.

In most instances, a snooker becomes more difficult to hit the closer the cue-ball is to the ball that is acting to obstruct a path to the object-ball. Diagram 11 shows a snooker that has been laid with only the blue, pink and black on the table. The blue has been cleverly doubled off the right-hand side cushion behind the pink and black which are close together at the top end of the table.

Although this shot undoubtedly demands a high level of skill, the snooker is straightforward enough to hit. The

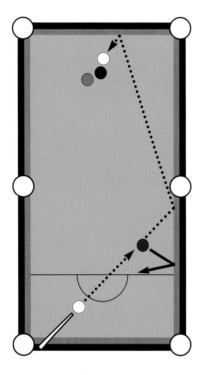

⑫ The better choice of shot is to clip off the blue and take the cue-ball off the right-hand cushion, tightly in behind the pink and black, leaving the next player with greater problems in making contact with the blue.

opportunity. Other veterans who fall into this category are Terry Griffiths, Dennis Taylor and Doug Mountjoy, all of whom are better potters than Rex.

ESCAPE FROM SNOOKERS

It is as important to be able to escape successfully from snookers as is it to lay them. Some snookers are harder to escape from than others, but it is only in exceptional cases that a player finds it impossible to fathom out a route to make contact with the ball 'on'. A player can escape from a snooker either by swerving the cue-ball or by striking it off one or more cushions. Obviously the second option requires a certain knowledge of angles and the way the cue-ball tends to leave the cushion. From this it follows that escapes which involve a number of cushions are usually more difficult to calculate than single-cushion escapes.

If there is only one cushion involved and the cue-ball and object-ball are close together, an experienced player should not have too much trouble in completing his escape. If you miss this type, or indeed any type of snooker, it is because you have either applied too much, too little or unwanted sidespin to the cue-ball, or quite simply misjudged the place on the cushion that you needed to hit. Diagram 13 shows the basic guideline to follow when attempting a straightforward one-cushion escape. Note the relative position of the cue-ball and object-ball and pick out the point on the cushion which is halfway between them. If you do this, the path of the cue-ball to and from the cushion will be V-shaped.

In many instances a much more complex escape is required, and to be consistently successful with these, a player has to learn from often bitter experience. I don't consider myself to be

better choice of shot is to clip off the blue and take the cue-ball off the right-hand side cushion, tightly in behind the pink and black (diagram 12). Now the next player to the table has greater problems in making contact with the blue.

When you require snookers to win a frame, it is generally more beneficial to lay one difficult snooker rather than ten that are easy to escape from. When I first turned professional, it didn't take me long to realise that the laying of snookers was one aspect of my game in which there was room for improvement. If I had to single out one player who has impressed me in this regard, it has to be Rex Williams, a former world billiards champion who uses his extensive knowledge of angles at every conceivable

'It is rarely impossible to fathom out a route to escape from a snooker.'

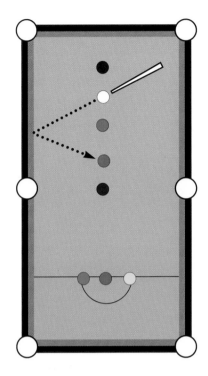

⓭ When attempting a one-cushion escape, note the relative position of the cue-ball and object-ball and pick out the point on the cushion which is halfway between them. The path of the cue-ball to and from the cushion will then be V-shaped.

a poor assessor of angles but, with all my knowledge, I still find some snookers extremely demanding.

Even if you are confident of hitting a snooker, there are other factors to take into consideration before you play it. It is important to work out where the object-ball will end up after the cue-ball has struck it. Remember, the primary function of a snooker is to force the victim into giving his opponent a scoring chance rather than penalty points. Sometimes I have hit a snooker and got a round of applause from the crowd, but not had another shot in the frame, as the escape has left my opponent the opportunity to make a decisive clearance.

Those of you who have a limited knowledge of the game's rules will, by now, be thinking to yourself that it is surely better to miss some snookers intentionally, on the basis that the penalty points you sacrifice by taking this course of action are an acceptable price

to pay for guaranteeing that the cue-ball comes to rest in a safe position. There are two reasons why it is not. First, it is against the rules and spirit of the game not to make a genuine attempt to hit the ball 'on'. I would have a very bad conscience and would certainly lose some self-esteem if I ever did this. Second, if the referee believes a player has not made a reasonable enough attempt to escape from a snooker, he calls a 'miss'.

This gives the non-offender three alternatives. He can play the shot from where the cue-ball lies, ask his opponent to play again from there, or tell the referee to replace the ball(s) in their original position. The offender then has to try to make a better escape attempt. If he does, the game continues normally, but if he does not satisfy the referee, the process is repeated indefinitely. The rule ensures that a snookered player cannot gain any advantage from a foul shot.

A rule which hangs on the judgement of a referee can cause controversy in any sport and snooker is no exception. Poor decisions are made, even by the top-class full-time referees that officiate on the professional circuit. However, for the most part, the rule achieves its aim and safeguards a player's chance of gaining a reward for a skilfully laid snooker.

Snooker purists enjoy witnessing clever safety battles as much as, if not more than, watching sizeable breaks. Potting and safety are complementary elements in snooker. Observation of more experienced players is the quickest way to learn the basics of safety play if you are a novice. Many players, including myself, have established a strong tactical game by carefully studying the approach to safety of more experienced players. Snooker can sometimes become akin to chess and you can get enormous pleasure from making the right moves.

10 THE MENTAL APPROACH

Only those who have played sport at a competitive level can fully understand the pressures and tension involved. At any level of snooker, a player's thought process can be vital in deciding the outcome of a match, with determination and single-mindedness often making the difference between two players of roughly the same ability.

People who take defeat lightly rarely make it to top level. On the other hand, those who become too annoyed with their own mistakes, and forfeit much of their composure as a result, will find it difficult to perform at their best. In the snooker clubs of Britain, you regularly hear of talented, yet temperamental, members who have smashed their cues in a rage. A balanced, strong mental approach is one of the most effective weapons a player can possess. To compete at the top, a player needs a combination of good technique and mental approach, for it is impossible to reach a high level without both.

One of the most damaging – and common – pitfalls that afflicts an inexperienced player in a competitive situation is to select, and play, shots at an unnatural pace. All players find their own tempo in practice and I have never understood why this rhythm should be abandoned during a match. I am neither a 'whirlwind' or a 'slow coach' and I like to think I play at the same speed in a match as I do when practising. There is a common misconception that more time should be taken in a match, yet if you start to hesitate and mull over every shot,

you will soon destroy your fluency and rhythm. Obviously everyone should have the gumption to consider certain key shots longer than normal, but it is pointless to ponder over straightforward shots. Conversely, those players who speed up under pressure and become careless will also suffer. The answer is to keep as closely as possible to your natural tempo and stick with it throughout, regardless of the state of the match.

To help you achieve this, a drill which is used on every shot could be introduced. Frank Callan, widely regarded as the top snooker coach in Britain, is a great advocate of 'the drill'. Certain professionals, such as Callan's long-time pupil Doug Mountjoy and Alan McManus, regulate their pace of play by going through a virtually identical routine on every shot. What you feel comfortable with is, of course, a personal matter, but there are a number of things to do to avoid mistakes creeping in.

You should always make your shot selection well before you put your bridge hand on the table in preparation to play it. It is therefore most important that you do not change your mind mid-stroke, so if you do have second thoughts and feel obliged to change your decision, you must get up from the shot and take up your revised stance from scratch. Finally, although I have to admit it is sometimes hard, never let the frame situation affect your outlook on a shot.

When I beat Jimmy White 18-14 in the final of the 1992 Embassy World Championship, there was one dead-weight pot on a brown that I will always remember. It came at an advanced stage of the 24th frame when I was trailing 14-9 and by 52 points. I knew it was a difficult shot but I also knew, if successful, it would lead to a clearance. It was a shot I thought I would pot, so with the minimum of hesitation I got down and potted it. I cleared up with 64 and went on to win the next eight frames. In 1985 Dennis Taylor potted the final black in the final frame of the World Championship to beat Steve Davis 18-17. If he had stood back, thought of the implications and treated with too much respect what was basically a simple pot, it is just possible that he might have made himself nervous enough to miss it.

If you do happen to make a costly error or have a devilish piece of luck run against you at a bad time, it is important to dismiss it from your mind. Again, this

> **'Although it is sometimes hard, never let the frame situation affect your outlook on a shot.'**

The courage to select and complete a difficult shot in the final of the 1992 World Championship led to victory over Jimmy White, and celebration with my girlfriend, Mandy, who is now my wife.

NEVER UNDERESTIMATE YOUR OPPONENT

● I CAN TELL YOU FROM RECENT PERSONAL EXPERIENCE THAT IT IS VERY DANGEROUS TO UNDERESTIMATE YOUR OPPONENT. IN THE 1993 UK CHAMPIONSHIP FINAL I DID JUST THAT AGAINST RONNIE O'SULLIVAN (RIGHT) — AND LOST 10-6. I WAS RIGHT TO BE CONFIDENT. I'D BEATEN RONNIE 6-2 IN THE SEMI-FINALS OF THE DUBAI CLASSIC SEVEN WEEKS EARLIER, AND TO BE HONEST HE HADN'T PLAYED ALL THAT WELL. IT WAS ALSO HIS FIRST MAJOR FINAL, HE WAS ONLY SEVENTEEN, AND I EXPECTED HIM TO BE OVERAWED BY IT ALL. IN ADDITION, I'D BROKEN A NUMBER OF RECORDS IN THE SEMI-FINALS DURING A 9-3 VICTORY OVER JOHN PARROTT. I SCORED 443 POINTS WITHOUT HIM POTTING A BALL AT ONE STAGE AND I MADE FIVE CENTURY BREAKS IN THE FIRST SESSION.

HOW WRONG I WAS TO UNDERESTIMATE RONNIE EVEN SLIGHTLY, BECAUSE HE HAD LEARNED FROM HIS DUBAI EXPERIENCE NOT TO BE SO OVERAWED BY ME OR AN OCCASION. IN ADDITION, EACH DAY IS DIFFERENT. I HAD PRODUCED A SPECIAL PERFORMANCE IN THE SEMI-FINAL, SO THE CHANCES WERE THAT I WOULDN'T PLAY QUITE AS WELL IN THE FINAL. EVEN IF THERE IS AN APPRECIABLE GAP IN ABILITY BETWEEN TWO PLAYERS, ONE HAS ONLY TO PLAY SLIGHTLY BETTER THAN USUAL ON THE DAY AND THE OTHER SLIGHTLY WORSE AND SUDDENLY THERE IS NO GAP LEFT.

is easier said than done. What you must do, if you are to make amends, is to accept that the shot is history and cannot be replayed. Don't punish yourself for a poor shot. You have not missed on purpose and every player, without exception, misses easy shots from time to time. Your attitude to your own mistakes is as important as your attitude to bad luck. It is no good saying: 'That's it, the gods are against me. I won't win now.'

The other aspect of a positive mental approach is the ability to play a shot on its merits, rather than consistently thinking about the strength or weakness of your opponent. In other words, do not let outside factors intrude; just play the balls. If you do not respect your opponent, you can become fatally over-confident and attempt a string of ambitious shots. If, however, you are frightened by the reputation of your opponent and become over-cautious in your approach, it is highly likely that you will not produce your best. Never become cocky or intimidated. If you see a pot and like the look of it, take it on. Never think: 'If I miss this, he'll step in and make a century break.'

NERVES, TENSION AND PRESSURE: HOW TO DEAL WITH THEM

In the 1989 Hong Kong Open, Dene O'Kane of New Zealand reached the final using meditation before his matches to soothe fraying nerves and relieve self-imposed pressure. Of course, not all players feel the need to employ such drastic measures to control tension, but it is a problem that afflicts almost everyone in varying degrees.

One of the most important victories a player can achieve over nervousness is simply to admit to its very existence. Don't think that by admitting to the effects of pressure you are somehow displaying a personality weakness, for if they are honest, all players will admit to having suffered from jangling nerve ends at one time or other. Some players are never able to free themselves in a competitive situation, and the disparity between their practice and match form is alarming. Even some of the top professionals would be much harder to beat if they didn't feel tension to such an extent.

The biggest and most harmful side-effect of nerves is a tendency for your cue-arm to tighten up so much that snatches result. A cue-arm full of tension makes a smooth delivery of the cue difficult and keeping yourself still on the shot nigh on impossible. Should your head, or indeed any other part of the upper body, move while a shot is being played, there is a significant likelihood that the shot will miss its intended target. If you begin to feel yourself falling under the influence of tension, it is imperative to make every effort to return to a more relaxed state of mind.

> **'If they are honest, all players will admit to having suffered from jangling nerve ends at one time or other.'**

One of the most frequent symptoms of pressure is for a player to grip his cue far more fiercely than is necessary. If you feel this happening, go about loosening

it and you will begin to feel more comfortable.

I know it is very easy to say that a player should always be positive and relaxed no matter what, but snooker just isn't like that. Certain circumstances are bound to generate a high degree of nervousness and, to be fair, there is little a player can do to combat it. When Franky Chan made his debut on British television against me at the 1991 Pearl Assurance British Open, he was particularly affected. I sensed this quickly and beat him 5-0.

At the start of my career the boot was on the other foot a number of times. For a while afterwards I used to get upset because the pressure of the situation had contributed to a number of unforced errors on my part. However, when the initial disappointment wore off, I put my defeat down to experience – or, in those cases, the lack of it – and I'm sure these

> **At any level of snooker, a player's thought process can be vital in deciding the outcome of a match.**

matches equipped me well for the future. If you do succeed in quelling nerves, your standard of matchplay will certainly improve. Obviously a certain amount of adrenalin is required – it does not pay to be too laid back – but nerves need to be coped with or your game will surely suffer.

How to Approach a Match

Practice is the most important factor in a player's preparation for a match, at whatever standard, but there are also several other factors to bear in mind. Most are plain common sense, although many a player has lost a match he should have won by breaking one or more of these ground rules of preparation.

It is important not to go into a match feeling bloated by a large meal eaten too recently. It makes you uncomfortable and any nutritionist will confirm that

excessive consumption of food dulls the senses. Snooker is a cerebral game and sharpness is essential if you are to compete at your best. That is why I can never understand why players, sometimes even professionals, drink alcohol before a match. They claim that, in moderation, alcohol soothes the nerves and consequently improves performance by being a relaxant. This is a dubious argument and my advice is to avoid alcohol consumption prior to a match. If you have a problem with a suspect temperament, you will find that conquering it from within will be much more satisfying – and lasting – than doing so with the help of an outside agent.

Never leave yourself in a situation where you have to waste nervous energy by rushing to a match and arriving a minute or two before the scheduled start. This is a sure way of wrecking your

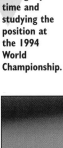

Taking my time and studying the position at the 1994 World Championship.

composure before a ball has been struck. Instead, prepare for a match in a sedate, relaxed manner. Give yourself plenty of time to reach the venue and you will feel the benefit. Obviously arriving too early gives time for you to become nervous, but there should always be time to become acclimatised to the surroundings and have a drink (non-alcoholic) before the contest commences. On the professional circuit Jimmy White often cuts his arrival fine, and while it does not appear to affect his game, Jimmy is very much an exception to this rule – and indeed several others.

'It's a great feeling when you are happy with your game and everything fits into place.'

Finally, I would urge all players, no matter what standard, to dress smartly when playing in a match. It is accepted that professionals, with their dress suit 'uniforms', always look their best. I am not suggesting that amateurs should dress like this for a first-round match in their club's individual tournament, but a smartly dressed player often has a psychological edge over a scruffy one if they are of roughly equal ability.

CONFIDENCE

However good you are, I'm sure you experience the odd frame or session in which you can do nothing wrong. It's a great feeling when you are happy with your game and everything fits into place.

When it happens to me, and it usually does about 10 per cent of the time, I make a string of century breaks, pull off virtually every shot I try and win frame after frame.

The only problem is that this state of mind does not last for ever and there is a

flip side of the coin. Even the leading professionals, myself included, go through periods when we can do nothing right. It's a crisis of confidence, a slump, and I can tell you that when it happens it's very worrying. Safety shots are misjudged, pots hit the jaws and wobble out instead of falling into the pocket and your positional play leaves plenty to be desired. Sometimes it's a technical fault, but on many occasions it's a simple lack of confidence.

At this point, you may be asking how someone with a talent for the game who practises six hours a day can suddenly lose his confidence. I can't explain why, but I can tell you that it happens.

In the weeks leading up to the 1994

When I'm going through a bad patch, I always try to play myself into form.

ETIQUETTE

● Snooker has a strong code of etiquette and the sportsmanship this helps to foster is, for me, one of the most appealing aspects of the game. All players carry some responsibility to enable these high standards of conduct to continue. Follow the following guidelines and you will quickly gain respect, not only as a player but also as a fair sportsman.

1. Shake hands with your opponent at the start and end of a match, regardless of the result. Don't rush off to sulk if you have lost, but congratulate your opponent if you have been beaten, or commiserate with him if you have won. Sometimes you may not want to do this, but in such a situation it pays to force yourself. It only takes a few seconds after all and is always worth it.

2. Shake hands with the referee at the start and finish of a match. In the amateur game his efforts, in a tough job, usually go unrewarded and it is wrong to take his services for granted. Likewise always try to make his life easy. Never argue with the referee, even if you think he has made a bad decision. In such an instance the best, and usually most productive, course of action is to ask the referee, very politely, to reconsider. Explain your thoughts in a controlled, composed manner. If, after your appeal, the decision is not changed, accept it with grace. However important the decision is in the context of a frame, it does not warrant an argument with the referee, which would be almost certain to shatter your concentration and composure.

Similarly, you should always declare your own fouls. If you nudge a red with your sleeve, it is sometimes undetectable by the referee. The player himself usually knows he has committed a foul of this nature and should always own up to it. As I have said before, dishonesty should not become part of a frame of snooker and players should strive to maintain high

Shaking hands with Jimmy White before the 1992 World Championship final.

standards of sportsmanship, so that for their own peace of mind, declaring fouls is the only thing to do. If you do get away with a breach of the rules, that little devil called guilt creeps into your thought processes and disturbs your concentration. I must admit to speaking from personal experience from my early days in the game when, like most other beginners, I did not fully appreciate the paramount importance of a strict etiquette in snooker.

3. Never do anything that is likely to affect your opponent's concentration, such as standing in his line of sight, making avoidable noises during his delivery of the cue, or moaning about the playing conditions while the match is still in progress. People who constantly complain about bad playing conditions, their own bad luck or the good fortune of their opponent can often adversely affect both their own concentration and his. They are a pet hate of mine, that's for sure.

World Championship, I was producing appalling snooker, both in practice and in matches. I lost to Tai Pichit, an amateur wild-card entry, in the first round of the Thailand Open and to Fergal O'Brien, then the world No. 100, in the quarter-finals of the Benson and Hedges Irish Masters. My concentration was terrible, I had a poor attitude and I made one blunder after another. Most of all, my confidence, normally one of my greatest assets, was at an all-time low.

In this situation, some players feel it's best to take a complete break from the game for a week or so, maintaining that confidence and staleness are linked and that a fresh start can work wonders. While this approach may help them, it's not for me. When I'm going through a bad patch, I always try to play myself back into form. I have to admit that sometimes you feel like your banging your head against a brick wall, but in my experience things come right in the end.

They certainly did for me in that World Championship run-up. After losing to Ronnie O'Sullivan in the semi-finals of the British Open, I returned home to practise for a week before travelling to the Crucible. I can't put my finger on why, but my form gradually came back. It was a great relief, I can tell you, and I arrived at the World Championship in a really optimistic frame of mind. It was a particularly satisfying feeling because I had battled through a bad spell.

PRACTICE – IT'S WORTH IT

So far in this book I have attempted to outline the technical and mental qualities needed to become a proficient snooker player. It is therefore appropriate that I should finish by discussing arguably the most important factor in producing a good player – practice. I don't know of one player – and I know an awful lot – who has become a competent player without spending many hours developing his game on the practice table. Practice, on a regular basis, is not only essential for improvement; it is virtually impossible to maintain your level of form without it.

During the close season there has always been a tendency for players to pack away their cues and take a rest. I have done this, but even if I have only two weeks off, I come back to find that the table appears to be double its normal

Practice is the most important factor in a player's preparation for a match.

help a player recover from a lack of confidence or combat a technical deficiency. If you have a problem, it pays to go back to the basics and check such key areas as stance, grip, bridge and cue action. As these are the very foundations on which the game of every individual is built, it pays to check whether they are in good working order. Very often the most aggravating of faults can be traced back to the basics.

As most people have a limited amount of time in which to practise, it is important to utilise that time to the full. There is little point in repeatedly practising your strong points. Instead, the shrewd player will strive to iron out particular bogey shots, which might be anything from screw shots to using the rest with any degree of accuracy. Practice does not guarantee that these bogey shots will become a player's strength, but if they are no longer a recognised weakness the objective has been achieved. Remember, too, that practice can drain your energy and concentration levels, so don't overdo it.

Too much practice can be almost as harmful to a player's game as too little. Solo practice sessions are invaluable, but I believe 100 per cent solo practice, to the exclusion of all else, can be harmful in that it does not allow a player to become acclimatised to the conditions he will face in a match. If you locked a

> SOME PLAYERS FIND IT DIFFICULT TO TRANSLATE PRACTICE FORM INTO THEIR MATCH PERFORMANCE. THE BEST EXAMPLE OF THIS IN THE PROFESSIONAL GAME IS MY GOOD MATE, WILLIE THORNE. HAVING PRACTISED WITH HIM QUITE A FEW TIMES AT TOURNAMENTS, I'M WELL QUALIFIED TO SAY WHAT A GREAT NATURAL TALENT HE POSSESSES, YET IN NINETEEN YEARS AS A PROFESSIONAL WILLIE HAS WON ONLY ONE WORLD RANKING EVENT — THE 1985 MERCANTILE CLASSIC.
> JIMMY WHITE TELLS ME TONY MEO, THE 1989 BRITISH OPEN CHAMPION, STILL POTS EVERYTHING IN SIGHT IN PRACTICE, BUT CAN'T SEEM TO REPRODUCE THAT CONSISTENCY IN A COMPETITIVE SITUATION.

length and width. Shots which are normally easy have to be treated with great respect and it takes a while to get rid of the rustiness. So it is easy for me to understand why people who have only a couple of frames per month find the game so difficult to master.

Those players amongst the amateur ranks who are sufficiently enthusiastic to devote a significant proportion of their leisure time to practice deserve, and usually get, their just reward. As snooker is like most other sports in that it gives back only what you put in, the dedicated players are always the ones who do best. Often I hear reluctant practice players excuse themselves by saying 'but I only play for pleasure'. The way I view it, there is little real pleasure in performing poorly.

Practice serves three main functions. It helps a player improve his game, it forms the preparation for a match, and it can

One of my regular practice partners is Billy Snaddon, a fellow professional from Scotland. Although we don't play for anything but pride, you wouldn't tell that from the intensity on our faces.

player away for ten years on his own and made him practise for ten hours a day every day, he would, of course improve. However, match conditions would be alien to him and it is unlikely that he would be able to cope with them without a period of readjustment.

Even though it is often serious, the fun part of practising is the playing of a number of frames with another player, and only by doing this can you ever hope to simulate match conditions. It is best to play a number of different opponents, for sticking with the same practice partner week in, week out, will almost inevitably lead to a certain staleness. Whenever possible, try to practise with a player of a higher standard than yourself.

much rarer breed of player who burn themselves out by practising too hard and at times, such as late at night, when they are unable to give 100 per cent concentration. Over-practising, which often leads to a player becoming obsessive about the theory of the game, can be highly counter-productive as it promotes staleness. Because of the concentration needed for snooker, a player's mind will cope effectively with only so much; after a certain point, when stale-ness sets in, a player's level of per-formance will usually drop. That said, the number of 'over-practisers' is out-weighed a hundred to one by those who do not practise enough.

'My experience of the game is that your standard largely determines the pleasure you get from it.'

One of my professional colleagues once said he wished he had a pound for every time someone had told him, 'I could have been a really good player if I had practised.' I immediately identified with what he had said, for the fact is that those unfulfilled players often chose not to practice. In snooker, as in life, you generally reap what you sow.

Snooker is a wonderful pastime for many people throughout the world, and my experience of the game is that your standard largely determines the pleasure you get from it. Many players have a life-long love affair with the green baize and continue to play well into their seventies or eighties. In this book I have tried to point new members of the snooker fold in the right direction. Take in and digest what you have read, start the correct way and you will have built a launchpad for rapid improvement. The rest is up to you. Good luck.

As well as providing a ready-made learn-ing process, the challenge of matching or even beating your 'superior' rival pro-vides a good incentive for improvement.

Most people who do not practise enough try to cover up by blaming luck, playing conditions, a lack of confidence or anything else that may spring to mind. Don't be like them, or indeed the

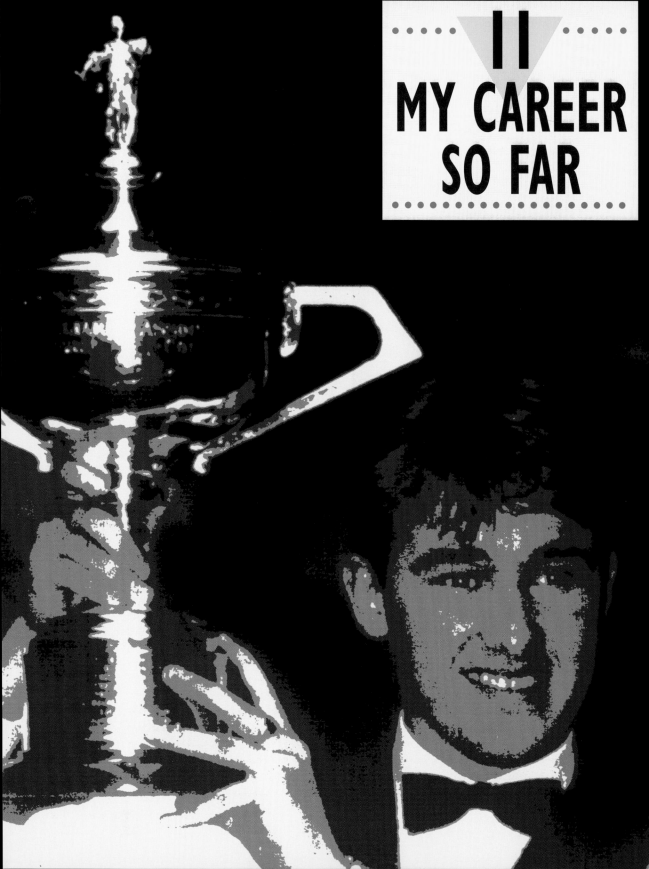

While most people remember a particular Christmas present, few have had their life moulded by one. I was thirteen when my parents bought me a miniature snooker table from John Menzies in Kirkcaldy on which I began to play a game that eventually became my profession.

Although in 1982 the snooker boom was in full swing, I was not that interested in the game. I can't say that watching Steve Davis win his second World Championship that year had the same effect on me as Jack Nicklaus's 1975 US Masters triumph had on Nick Faldo. I did not take up snooker as a result of being inspired; it just happened. After

only a couple of shots on my 6 x 3 table, I was captivated and my parents did not see much of me over that Christmas holiday. I was in another room potting balls.

By today's standards, I suppose I was a pretty late starter – Ronnie O'Sullivan made his first century break when he was ten – but I soon made up for lost time. I made a 50 break within a couple of weeks and then started playing on a full-size table, once a week, at Malocos Snooker Club, Dunfermline. All day, every day, I was playing on my own small table, but I really looked forward to those Monday-night experiments on a full-size one. In the beginning I was pretty useless, but that did not stop me wanting to go back for more.

I improved quickly and after a few months was playing virtually every day at the Classic Snooker Centre in Dunfermline. When I was fourteen, almost exactly a year to the day after I started playing on the miniature table, I compiled my first century break. I had another one the following day.

At the risk of sounding conceited, I have to admit that my improvement was meteoric. I won the Scottish Amateur Championship when I was fourteen, retained it the next year and qualified to represent my country in the 1984 World Amateur Championship in Dublin.

Looking back on it now, I can see I had a lot of ragged edges, but I'd also won the Scottish and British under-16 titles that year and I thought I could do well. In the end I finished third in my round-robin qualifying group and failed to reach the knockout stages.

> **'My life was moulded by the Christmas present my parents gave me when I was thirteen.'**

After qualifying for my Crucible debut in 1986, I gave Willie Thorne a scare in the first round.

By this time I was being managed by Ian Doyle, the Stirling businessman who was, and still is, one of the biggest influences on my career. We toyed with the idea of my retaining amateur status for another year to have a tilt at the 1985 World Amateur Championship, scheduled for Blackpool, but decided against it in favour of turning professional.

In those days, before qualifying schools and then 'open' snooker were introduced, a player wishing to become a professional had to apply to the game's governing body, the World Professional Billiards and Snooker Association. Largely because I had won the Scottish Amateur Championship twice, my application was accepted.

'Even though I was only eighteen and he was the world No.1, Steve Davis treated me with the utmost respect, as he does all his opponents.'

I can tell you that the learning process as a rookie professional can be a painful one, and it certainly was for me at times during that first season. Like when I was hammered 9-2 by O. B. Agrawal, of India, in a qualifying round for the 1985 UK Championship – one of his rare wins as a professional. Worse was to come.

My manager, astutely realising that the experience would do me the world of good, arranged a six-night exhibition tour around Scotland in February 1987 with Steve Davis. Ian knew that it was a case of learning the hard way, because Steve gave me a drubbing I'll never forget. In front of one capacity crowd after another, Steve gave me beating after beating. In the end the final score of the series was 39-15, but to me it felt more like 100-0. Halfway through that tour I felt so inadequate that I felt like quitting the game.

Now I realise that going through the mincer in public like that was invaluable. Even though I was only eighteen Steve, then the reigning world champion and world No. 1, treated me with the utmost respect, as he does all his opponents. It made me appreciate that in snooker attitude and application are as important as ability.

During that season there were times when I did not practise enough, or when my attitude to what I regarded as 'easy' matches was completely wrong. Ian and I had a number of arguments because of this – and of course he was right. After losing so heavily to Steve, the message that Ian had been trying to convey finally began to sink in. The same applies to all players: ability is no good in isolation. Only with practice and the right approach can a player make the most of his potential.

Thanks to Steve and Ian, I turned a psychological corner. It was not as if I had not had any success. The previous year, shortly after my seventeenth birthday, I became the youngest-ever winner of a professional tournament when I beat Matt Gibson 10-5 in the final of the Scottish Championship.

That was a big thrill, as was my qualification for the final, televised, stages of the 1986 Embassy World Championship. I beat four tough opponents to earn my Crucible debut, in which I gave Willie Thorne a real fright before losing 10-8 in the first round. While it was a big disappointment to lose so narrowly, I acquitted myself well and felt a whole lot better about my prospects for the new season than I had a few months earlier. Even so, it was that lesson from Steve which made me realise I wasn't playing to my potential.

The 1986-87 campaign was one in which my improvement continued and a

In terms of personal satisfaction, the 1987-88 season turned out to be an A+.

Until then, it was not just those wins over me on our Scottish tour which gave Steve Davis an aura of invincibility in my eyes. He also beat me 9-3 in the semi-final of the 1987 Mercantile Classic and by the same score in the final of that year's Hong Kong Masters. So you can imagine my satisfaction when I beat Steve 5-2 in the last sixteen of the 1987 Rothmans Grand Prix. It was only a best-of-nine-frame match, but finally beating Steve was a great feeling. I got as much elation from it as I did from winning the world title for the first time. It was that important to me.

In fact, I went on to beat Tony Knowles in the quarter-finals, John Parrott in the semis and Dennis Taylor in the final to become, at eighteen years and nine months, the youngest-ever winner of a ranking event. That record was broken in November 1993 when Ronnie O'Sullivan beat me in the final of the UK Championship when he was still a week short of his eighteenth birthday. I can only say that if Ronnie gained as much from his breakthrough as I did from mine, he must have been brimming with confidence. From being a pretender to the crown of Steve Davis, I became convinced I could be the best.

The 1987 World Championship was especially memorable for my exciting quarter-final against the reigning champion, Joe Johnson.

time when I consolidated my position as the circuit's leading prospect. I retained the Scottish professional title, reached the semi-finals of a ranking event for the first time at the Mercantile Classic, and again qualified for the Crucible, losing 13-12 to Joe Johnson in a quarter-final which remains one of the most exciting matches I've ever been involved in.

If I had been at school, I think my report card at the end of that season would have read: Stephen has shown encouraging signs but can do better – B.

I was so motivated and focused that I practised more and more in an effort to get to the top of the rankings. It was not just the quantity but the quality of my practice time that improved. I mixed a fair amount of solo practice with frames against other good players in the Spencers Snooker Club in Stirling and I benefited greatly.

If you are a club player who, reading this, thinks you have little in common with a leading professional, then think again. As I've said before in this book, the same principles apply to us all. Getting the most out of practice is vitally important.

Most of you who are working during the day will feel quite tired at night. If this is the case, my advice would be to limit your evening practice, because it can be counter-productive to play when concentration is difficult to summon. If you do not put everything into it, practice is not worth a jot. Just banging the ball around aimlessly does a player no good whatsoever. The same is true for playing against a lesser player than yourself. It's OK knocking in breaks all day long, but only by playing against a player of equal or higher standard can you hone your competitive skills and become match sharp.

By the beginning of 1988, with the Grand Prix title tucked under my belt, a sensible practice routine in place and bundles of confidence, I was ready to begin my final assault on the game's

'The same principles apply to us all, from club player to professional.'

upper slopes. It was to take me two years to reach the summit.

I did enough in 1988 to secure my place in the world's top sixteen for the first time, winning the Scottish Championship for the third year in succession and adding the New Zealand Masters title, but the highlight of my year as a 13-2 victory over Mike Hallett in the British Open final.

One of the perks of being in the 'elite' top sixteen is an automatic invitation to the Benson and Hedges Masters at Wembley Conference Centre, an event rightly regarded as snooker's most prestigious invitation tournament. From the first time I played in the vast 2,600 seat auditorium in 1989, I felt both comfortable and inspired. I beat John Parrott 9-6 to win the title and start a five-year unbeaten sequence in the event.

My run stretched for 23 matches until the 1994 final, when I lost 9-8 to Alan McManus. Yet, in the 1991 final, only a mad man would have thought I was going to win the Masters for a third year in a row when I trailed Mike Hallett 7-0 and 8-2.

Having partnered Mike to victory in the World Doubles Championship and the men's doubles at the World Masters, I knew his game better than most. I was

My manager Ian Doyle, has been, and still is, one of the biggest influences on my career.

fully aware that he was unstoppable at times and when he went six up with seven to play, I thought my goose was cooked. However, I also knew that Mike had never won a major title in Britain and that he'd be anxious to get over the winning line. I figured that if I could put him under a bit of pressure by winning the next two frames, I stood an outside chance.

My theory about Mike feeling tense was confirmed when he started committing unforced errors. The burden of pressure was squarely on his shoulders and, with the passing of each frame, I could see it was getting heavier. Any player who can pick up signs about how his opponent is feeling is obviously at an advantage. It's worth a lot, so always try to keep an eye on your rival's reactions.

Mike's game fell apart, I had some

luck at the right time and, in front of a television audience on BBC which was double that for the men's singles final at that year's Wimbledon, I fought back to win 9-8. It remains one of my most memorable results.

Apart from launching my monopoly in the Benson and Hedges Masters, I won four other tournaments in 1989. They were the Asian Open, the Regal Scottish Masters, the Dubai Classic and, most significantly of all as far as I was concerned, the UK Championship. In the final at Preston Guild Hall, I played some of my finest snooker to beat Steve Davis 16-12. I didn't know it at the time, but that victory was to give me a lot of self-belief going into the following year's Embassy World Championship.

While 1989 was good to me, 1990 was even better. In addition to retaining

In 1989 I won the first of five consecutive Benson and Hedges Masters titles.

the Scottish Masters, Benson and Hedges Masters, Asian Open and Dubai Classic titles, I also beat Nigel Bond 10-5 in the final of the Rothmans Grand Prix to win that event for the second time.

But overshadowing everything else was my success in the World Championship. When I beat Jimmy White 18-12 to capture the game's most coveted title, I realised an ambition I'd had since those days spent potting balls on my miniature table at home. The press kept reminding me that, at twenty-one years and three months, I had superseded Alex Higgins – aged twenty-three when he won in 1972 – as

After winning my second Rothmans Grand Prix in 1990, I went on to take my first world title and finished the year ranked No.1.

the youngest-ever world champion. Although that was definitely something to be proud of, there was a more significant side issue in my mind.

I had enjoyed such a successful season that I had finally taken over from Steve as the world No. 1. I've gone on record many times since as saying that being top of the rankings is more important to me than being world champion, and I really believe it is. The world champion may receive more exposure, but being No. 1 is a true sign of consistency. I suppose the analogy at amateur level is the guy who wins the individual event of a particular local league, as opposed to the player who has the most wins in the highest division. In my opinion the latter achievement is more noteworthy.

Having reached No. 1 for the 1990-91 season, I was determined not to rest on my laurels. I won seven major tournaments, lost in the final of two others and smashed one of the game's long-standing records in the process. From my first round in the 1990 World Championship to the final of the 1991 Mercantile Credit Classic, when I lost 10-4 to Jimmy White, I won 36 consecutive matches in world ranking events. Normally records do not mean that much to me, but this one did.

Ronnie O'Sullivan has since broken it with a run of 38 unbeaten matches. However, they were all in the qualifying rounds of events in the summer of 1992, and although this was a great effort by Ronnie, especially considering they were his first 38 matches as a professional, he was not meeting top-class opposition in front of the television cameras, as I was in my unbeaten sequence.

What I did not anticipate was that all these victories would contribute to my failure when it mattered most, for I arrived at the World Championship

I may not have won the World title in 1991, but being No.1 was more important to me.

suffering from a degree of competitive burn-out and paid the price. My hopes of becoming the only player other than Steve Davis to successfully defend the title since the Crucible became the Championship's permanent home in 1977 were dashed when I lost 13-11 to Steve James in the quarter-finals.

In total contrast to me, John Parrott, who had enjoyed little success in the second half of the season, arrived in Sheffield refreshed and ready for the seventeen-day battle ahead. He played superbly and won a title his talent richly deserves by beating Jimmy White 18-11 in the final.

After my initial disappointment had abated, I digested the result, looked for causes and realised that, in some ways, I had been the victim of my own success. I decided that I would need to be

mentally stronger, because there was no way I wanted to cut down on competitive appearances just in order to be sharp for the World Championship.

Again I increased my practice workload, up to as much as eight hours a day, and the dividends were reaped during the 1991-92 campaign, in a season which remains one of my most profitable, both in terms of titles and prize money. In all I won eight tournaments, I regained the world title and, as icing on the cake, I compiled a maximum break in the Matchroom League. The financial consequence of this was a prize-money total for the season of £645,300. I was also pretty pleased with the £694,056 I had collected the previous season

When I trailed Jimmy White 14-8 in the final of the World Championship everyone except me thought that, at last, Jimmy was finally going to rid himself of an unwanted reputation as the best player never to win the game's blue riband event. I knew I was cueing well enough to make a comeback and, aided by a couple of mistakes from Jimmy, that's what I did.

After winning a scrappy 23rd frame, I let Jimmy in for a 52 break in the next. He missed a red with the rest, though, and I eventually put together a 64 break to trail only 10-14 going into the final session. The key shot in that clearance came when I left the cue-ball stuck in the jaws of the middle pocket.

'The 1991-92 season remains one of my most profitable, both in terms of titles and prize money.'

I could have potted a straight blue, but position on the yellow, which was close to the baulk cushion, would have been impossible. Although I knew it was not the percentage shot, I potted the brown at dead weight to a baulk pocket and held position for the yellow.

It was the ultimate pressure shot, because if I'd missed it Jimmy would surely have cleared up to lead 15-9. It was one of those instances, which you will undoubtedly come across, where you fancy a particular shot and defy conventional wisdom by taking it on.

I have to say that attempting too many of these extremely risky pots is wrong, because sooner rather than later you'll come unstuck – and I speak from bitter experience. However, it sometimes pays to play a hunch, as it did for me on that occasion.

I dominated the concluding session, winning all eight frames and finishing off in style with breaks of 134 and 112. Again, like the 1991 Benson and Hedges Masters final when I fought back against Mike Hallett, I drew confidence from picking up on Jimmy's signs of frustration and concern. By the end he was understandably demoralised while, to me, the pockets looked like buckets.

Although I felt sorry for Jimmy in one respect, I can tell you the boot's been on the other foot a few times. As I mentioned before, he won nine frames on the trot when he beat me 10-4 in the 1991 Mercantile Classic final and I was trounced 9-2 by him in the semi-finals of that year's UK Championship. Every year I desperately want to win the world title, but if it is not to be mine, then I would love to see Jimmy's name engraved on the trophy. He has shown time and again that, in addition to being an inspirational player, he is a true sportsman and gracious loser.

It came as something of an unpleasant shock when, six months into the 1992-93 season, I was still waiting to win my first event. I lost deciding-frame finishes

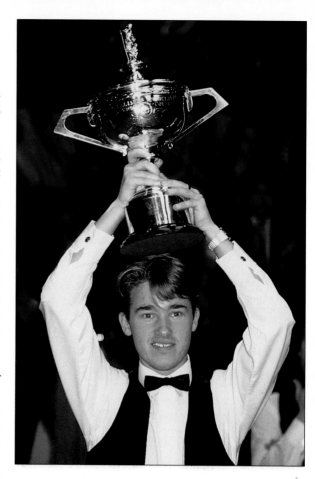

to John Parrott in the Kent Classic in Peking and the Dubai Classic, and it was particularly annoying because I knew that, in practice, I was playing as well as ever.

The elusive first title came at the European Challenge in France, and although it was only a small eight-man invitation tournament, the win nevertheless restored a measure of my lost confidence. I went on to win the Benson and Hedges Masters for the fifth year in succession – the sponsors gave me the gold trophy to keep this time – but the biggest boost to my morale came at the International Open, the first ranking event covered by Sky Sports.

During my six matches at the Plymouth Pavilion I made ten century breaks, the most ever by one player in a world ranking tournament. That, and a

My triumph in the 1992 World Championship was followed by a six-month period in which I won no title.

10-6 victory over my old adversary Steve Davis in the final, was the perfect tonic with the World Championship just a couple of weeks away. I maintained that kind of form at the Crucible and won the world title for the third time by beating Jimmy again, 18-5 in the final. The 1993-94 season began in encouraging fashion when I won the Dubai Classic and European Open. That latter success made me the first player to win all nine world ranking events at least once. However, things began to go wrong in February, when I lost to Alan McManus in both the quarter-finals of the Regal Welsh Open and the final of the Benson and Hedges Masters. That shattered my 100 per cent record at Wembley and, to be honest, I felt a little deflated.

'My greatest weakness is an occasional lack of motivation.'

When people ask me if I have a weakness, I always say that my worst fault is an occasional lack of motivation, which usually strikes when I'm playing a little-known player in the early rounds of a tournament. My Achilles' heel helped me come a cropper the following month.

After Alan beat me in the Masters, he whitewashed me 5-0 in the quarter-finals of the International Open. Such a drubbing should have made me all the more determined when I travelled to the Thailand Open in Bangkok, where I was due to play Tai Pichit, a local wild-card

entry in the last 32. Yet I took him too lightly, even though he was the reigning world amateur champion, and lost 5-2 in what many of the papers, both in Britain and in Thailand, described as the biggest upset in snooker history. While I would dispute that on the grounds that Pichit is an accomplished player, it certainly was a major setback for me.

Steve Davis, who won the Regal Welsh Open, reached the final of the Thailand Open a week after I had flown home to Scotland and suddenly he was back on top of the provisional world rankings for the first time since 1990.

I had encountered a similarly barren spell at the start of the previous season, but this was much more worrying. Then, I was unable to achieve the desired results in matches, despite playing well in practice; this time I was struggling in practice as well as in matches.

My confidence was further dented by a 5-2 quarter-final defeat by Fergal O'Brien in the Benson and Hedges Irish Masters and a 6-2 loss to Ronnie O'Sullivan in the semi-finals of the British Open. Having displayed such poor form, I did not regard the World

After another barren spell in 1994, I was relieved to rediscover my self-belief in time for the World Championship.

Championship as an enticing prospect. All I could do was to continue practising hard and hope against hope that my game would improve. I knew there was not a technical problem and that it was simply a matter of self belief. Thankfully, in the week leading up to the Championship I started to feel comfortable again.

I won my opening match against Surinder Gill 10-1 and when I established a 7-1 lead over Dave Harold, the 1993 Asian Open champion, I felt very satisfied. I went to a local Chinese restaurant, had a quiet meal and elected to have a nice early night. Then disaster struck.

Coming out of the bathroom in my hotel suite, I slipped on the wet floor and my left arm took the weight of my whole

> **'All I could do was to continue practising hard and hope against hope that my game would improve.'**

body as I fell. It was a little painful at the time, but I thought nothing of it as I went to sleep. On waking the following morning I could think of nothing else.

I was in agony and a specialist at a local hospital confirmed my worst fears: I had sustained a hairline fracture just below my left elbow. The doctor drained some blood away from the injury, which eased the pain considerably, and he also gave me a course of anti-inflammatory tablets. After an extremely trying morning, I was very relieved when I was given the all clear to continue playing.

By this time the story had broken, the accident was common knowledge and I was the centre of attention. When the match resumed it did not help that, apart from the discomfort I was still feeling, my head was full of doubts about how I was going to play.

Anyone who watched that session on television will know that I lost the opening frame of the afternoon and cued very gingerly in the process. After a few shots, though, I began to realise that in situations where I required a normal bridge I was not too severely handicapped. Knocking in a 124 break in the second frame of the session also helped considerably, and I went on to win the following five frames to record a 13-2 victory and win with a full session to spare.

In one respect, at least, I was lucky because I play with a bent bridge arm, which meant that the injury did not compromise my natural style. Unfortunately, the same could not be said when I applied pressure to the fracture by bridging with the fingers on a cushion or when I had to lift my bridge to contend with intervening balls.

Even though I beat Nigel Bond 13-8 in the quarter-finals, the pain from my arm had intensified to such an extent that I made a return visit to the hospital to see if, by playing, I had aggravated the injury. After re-examining me, the doctor said that there was no further damage but advised me to rest the arm by putting it in a sling between matches.

The photographers down at the Crucible had a field day but, although I smiled for them, I can tell you that inside I was feeling terrible. Because of the sling, I knew I would not be able to practise for more than half an hour the following day, when one of the biggest matches of my career was to begin.

My opponent was Steve Davis and we renewed our rivalry with more than a place in the world final at stake. The winner would be guaranteed top spot in the rankings for the following season. To me that meant an awful lot. We both

Despite the handicap of a fractured left arm, I beat Steve Davis to retain the No.1 ranking and overcame Jimmy White 18-17 in the final to take my fifth world title.

championship final, 7-9. I'd fought a constant battle to keep my concentration, because the pain from the fracture was still nagging away, and my potting from under the cushions was considerably impaired. I need not have worried on this score. The adrenalin that all players experience on big occasions, be it the final of the club championship or, in the case, the final of the World Championship, enabled me to forget my discomfort when the last two sessions were played. There is also no doubt in my mind that being involved in such a dramatic match helped greatly in keeping me focused.

The initiative ebbed and flowed until the deciding frame when Jimmy, in prime position, missed a straightforward black and I put together a 58 clearance to win 18-17. It was

made mistakes in the early stages — understandably considering the importance of the contest — but from 8-9 I won eight frames in succession as, to my surprise, Steve committed a series of uncharacteristic errors. I won 16-9 and felt an overwhelming sense of relief.

By retaining the world No. 1 position, I had achieved my revised primary objective after breaking the arm. With four sessions to play over two days, I looked on victory in the final as no more than an added bonus.

After the first day, I trailed Jimmy White, appearing in his sixth world

a miss, a clearance, a result and a match I will always remember. When the dust had settled, I was asked by a lot of journalists whether I thought breaking the modern era record of six world titles jointly held by Ray Reardon and Steve Davis was a realistic proposition. I did not hesitate in providing a positive answer.

I still love snooker, I love my lifestyle and I love being at the top of my profession. I will carry on playing as long as I think I can win any tournament I enter. I am not satisfied with merely reaching the semi-finals or final of an event: to me that is failure.

Another good reason for my continued enthusiasm is that I firmly believe there is room for improvement in my game. For two years I was coached by Frank Callan, who helped me immensely by giving me knowledge of my own game.

Thanks to Frank, I'm able to dissect every part of it if anything goes wrong. At the moment I've come to realise that, on occasions, my shot selection can be poor. Unlike Steve Davis, I've lost out in the past because, when I've been playing poorly, I have not been able to adapt my shot selection accordingly. In months and years to come there will undoubtedly be other aspects of my game with which I am not satisfied and which require attention.

Even as world champion I know I can improve my standard. So can you, of course, and I sincerely hope that this book will allow you to do just that.

THE MAXIMUM AND WHAT IT MEANT

To have a maximum in practice is very pleasing; to make one in a match – like I did against Willie Thorne in the 1992 Matchroom League – is a great feeling. But I can tell you that making one at the Crucible is the ultimate.

When I arrived in Sheffield for the 1995 Championship, my main objective was to retain my world title, but it has always been a big ambition of mine to knock in a 147 in front of the television cameras. Only five other players have achieved that distinction, and although I'd had some chances to do it, every one of them slipped through my fingers.

My best chance came at the 1994 International Open. It was a last 16 match against Tony Drago, and when I got down to just the last four colours, I genuinely thought I was going to pick up the keys to a Rolls-Royce Silver Spirit that my sponsors, Team Sweater Shop, had offered any of our management stable for making a televised 147 that season. However, my hopes were shattered, because I over-screwed off the brown and left myself a virtually impossible cut on the blue using the long rest.

The last thing on my mind when I began my semi-final against Jimmy was a maximum. He might have had a terrible season, but he's always a very dangerous opponent and therefore winning was no formality.

Halfway through the second session I led 7-4. I'd just put together a 119 clearance and was full of confidence, so that when the chance for the 147 arrived in the twelfth frame, I was mentally equipped to grab it.

Of course, there were crunch moments – there always are in a break like that – but while I was nervous towards the end, I didn't let it affect my cueing or, indeed, my thinking. I knew it was important to keep the right tempo

'The feeling on making a maximum is pure elation, because for one frame you've achieved perfection.'

and not to rush or become too hesitant.

Whenever I'd seen videos of Cliff Thorburn dropping on his knees after his 147 at the Crucible in 1983, or of Kirk Stevens embracing all and sundry after his maximum at the following year's Benson and Hedges Masters, I always wondered what they must have been feeling. Now, from first-hand experience, I can tell you that it is pure elation; and in some respects it's better than winning a tournament, because for one frame you've attained perfection.

One of the journalists told me the break had taken just over eleven minutes

My opponent in the final of the 1995 World Championship was my Team Sweater Shop stablemate Nigel Bond.

who was commentating on the match, described it as 'the greatest frame of snooker' he'd ever seen. Be that as it may, it was certainly one I'll never forget.

The 1994-95 season was generally kind to me, even if I did have some major set-backs. Losing 9-8 to Peter Ebdon in the final of the Benson and Hedges Irish Masters after I had been 4-0, 5-1 and 8-6 ahead was not the best experience. The same applied to my surprise 5-4 first-round defeat in the Sweater Shop International Open by Mark Johnston-Allen.

But, once again, the highs far outweighed the lows, and I finished the season with another string of record-breaking feats to my name.

I won the Top Rank Classic in Thailand – a curtain-raiser to the new campaign – but for the next couple of months I was in something of a slump. All that changed at the UK Championship in Preston. When I trailed Dean Reynolds 8-4 in the last 32 it looked like another early exit, but I battled hard, stole one frame on a re-spotted black and eventually scraped through 9-8. It was the turning point I'd been desperate for.

After that I began to play with my old confidence and in the final I made no less than seven century breaks during my 10-5 victory over Ken Doherty. That, apart from being a record, was the best standard of play I'd ever produced in a match. My total of century breaks for the Championship as a whole was twelve, itself a record by one player in a world ranking event.

to compile. It seemed much longer to me, and that's why I was so proud I held myself together.

The commotion the break caused was unbelievable. The crowd raised the roof and when I got backstage I realised what a big story it would be in the following day's newspapers.

Of course the BBC were delighted. CNN, the worldwide news network based in Atlanta, Georgia, used my final black as their sports programme's 'Play of the Day' and Phil Yates even did a live commentary on the last few colours for radio, would you believe?

The response from everyone was fantastic. I received a lot of congratulatory telegrams, including one from Alex Ferguson and all at Manchester United. That was a nice thought.

When that final black fell in, I had earned a £147,000 bonus from Embassy, as well as the Championship's £16,000 highest-break prize. Someone told me later that during the course of the break I'd earned about £230 a second.

Of course the money was great, but the feeling – well, that was priceless. John Spencer, a former world champion

In December, I retained the European Open title – my fiftieth tournament success as a professional – and then in January I beat Dennis Taylor 9-1 to win the inaugural Liverpool/Victoria Charity Challenge.

Everything was going so well until I lost 5-1 to my fellow Scot, Chris Small, in the quarter-finals of the Regal Welsh Open and 5-4 to Ebdon at the same stage of the Benson and Hedges Masters at Wembley.

Suddenly I couldn't do anything right, even though in practice I was playing better than ever. Luckily, when I arrived at the Crucible, attempting to win the World Championship for an unprecedented fourth year in succession, things went my way. I have only to step into that place and I get all charged up. That's what I need most of all, because the more you do in any walk of life, particularly in sport, the harder it is to become motivated and inspired.

'However I'm feeling beforehand, I have only to step into the Crucible and I get all charged up.'

After beating Crucible newcomer Stefan Mazrocis and Tony Drago fairly comfortably in the opening two rounds, I came up against Ronnie O'Sullivan in the quarter-finals. Ronnie has more talent in his little finger than 99 per cent of players have in their whole body. He had won the Masters in February and, only a couple of weeks before, had been runner-up to John Higgins in the British Open.

That, and the fact that he'd played superbly to beat me 5-2 in the previous month's Thailand Open, made me appreciate just how tough this match was going to be. So it proved as Ronnie, refusing to be shaken off, trailed only 9-8, but I responded to the challenge with breaks of 88, 84 and 133 on the way to winning 13-8. I had answered a lot of questions with that burst and became convinced that world title number five was just around the corner.

Jimmy White, my opponent in the semi-final, had been through a nightmare season with his off-table problems mirroring those he had endured on it. I wasn't expecting him to push me too hard, I have to admit, but Jimmy conjured up his best form in a long time.

Making the 147 in the second session (see my section on the maximum) was fantastic, but it only secured one frame and Jimmy refused to throw in the towel. In many ways it was like the O'Sullivan match all over again. Jimmy won three frames on the trot to trail only 14-12 before I stepped on the gas in the next two. He didn't score another point as I completed victory with breaks of 72 and 100. Nigel Bond, my Team Sweater Shop stablemate, had booked his place in the final by beating the likes of Alan

The highlight on the road to my fifth world title in 1995 was the maximum I made in the semi-final against Jimmy White.

McManus, Gary Wilkinson and, in the semi-finals, Andy Hicks, so there was no way I was going to take anything for granted, even if the bookmakers installed me as a 1-12 favourite.

After the first session Nigel deservedly led 4-3, but in the second he committed a lot of mistakes. I punished them, led 11-5 overnight, and on day two of the final, feeling relaxed, I pulled way to win 18-9.

While the final was nothing like as dramatic as the previous year's against Jimmy, I felt more drained of emotion. What with the 147, beating Ronnie, Jimmy and retaining the title, it had been

a memorable few days.

Later, I was informed that during the final I'd broken my own record for century breaks by one player in a season and had set a new record by constructing twelve centuries during a Championship at the Crucible. That was another source of considerable satisfaction.

My Championship pay packet was yet another record. I collected a £190,000 first prize, £147,000 for the maximum and £16,000 for the highest break: a grand total of £353,000, which I'm sure you'll agree is not bad.

My total number of centuries for the season was swelled to fifty-three by the

STEPHEN HENDRY'S LIST OF MAJOR TITLES

RANKING TOURNAMENTS

1987 – Rothmans Grand Prix
1988 – MIM Britannia British Open
1989 – 555 Asian Open, Dubai Duty Free Classic, Stormseal UK Championship
1990 – Embassy World Championship, Rothmans Grand Prix, 555 Asian Open, Dubai Duty Free Classic, Stormseal UK Championship
1991 – Pearl Assurance British Open, Rothmans Grand Prix
1992 – Regal Welsh Open, Embassy World Championship
1993 – Sky Sports International Open, Embassy World Championship, Dubai Classic, European Open (December)
1994 – Embassy World Championship, European Open, UK Championship
1995 – Embassy World Championship

OTHER TITLES

1986 – Scottish Professional Championship
1987 – Scottish Professional Championship
1988 – Scottish Professional Championship, New Zealand Masters
1989 – Benson and Hedges Masters, Regal Scottish Masters
1990 – Benson and Hedges Masters, Regal Scottish Masters
1991 – Benson and Hedges Masters, 555 Challenge (Hong Kong), 555 Challenge (Delhi), Matchroom League
1992 – European Challenge, Benson and Hedges Masters, Benson and Hedges Irish Masters, Matchroom League
1993 – Benson and Hedges Masters, Canal Plus European Challenge
1994 – Matchroom League, Top Rank Classic
1995 – Liverpool/Victoria Charity Challenge, Matchroom League

quartet of 100-plus contributions I had in winning the following week's Matchroom League. That was worth another £50,000 and it boosted my tournament earnings for the season to £740,500.

I know I'm fortunate. Snooker has been really good to me; it's given me countless hours of pleasure and financial security. Not everyone can be world champion or even a professional, but that doesn't stop you making the most of what is a cracking game.

My Maximum and How it was Achieved

It's very rare to make a total clearance without having to develop reds from the pack, and this was no exception.

I had already potted five reds with five blacks when I was presented with the opportunity to bring out some more. There was always the possibility of the cue-ball getting stuck in the reds and having its pace taken away, but I thought that losing position was a small risk.

The pot itself wasn't difficult, and when the reds fanned nicely and I dropped perfectly on the black, I knew a 147 was there for the taking.

If there was a negative aspect to the shot, it was a lone red which travelled up past the middle pocket. That would pose a problem in the latter stages of the break. I kept the red that carried towards the baulk end of the table until last. Off the fourteenth black I played a pretty good positional shot to be able to pot the red to the green pocket.

The pot itself wasn't too much of a problem, but I had to play it with stun and right-hand side to get the cue-ball on to the black. An added complication was a need to avoid kissing the blue and pink, which were close together in the middle of the table.

The last red went in, and after that the crowd began to cheer every shot. I have to admit my legs were like jelly after I sank the fifteenth black and obtained ideal position on the yellow.

The unfortunate run I'd encountered early in the frame was nudging the pink too close to the blue for comfort. I couldn't cut it into either middle pocket because the pink was blocking its path to both, so I had to settle for potting it to the distant yellow pocket.

By this time my nerve ends were really jangling, but I was determined to cue it sweetly and remember to avoid breaking any rule of good technique. I can tell you I was relieved when the blue grazed the near jaw and fell.

Part two of the shot was also successful: I had played a soft stun to kiss the pink closer to a middle pocket. It worked a treat and the pot was easy.

Unfortunately, while potting the pink was simple enough, taking the cue-ball off side and baulk cushions fully sixteen feet back to position on the black required fairly precise judgement. Maybe because of the adrenalin rush I was experiencing, I over-hit the cue-ball and finished almost touching the top cushion. A quarter of an inch further into the table and I'm sure it would have been the natural angle to take the cue-ball in-off in the middle pocket.

As it was, I settled myself over what was quite an acute cut back and tried to empty my head of negative thoughts. When I played the stroke it felt good, and I was even more confident I'd potted one of the most satisfying shots of my career when a couple of members of the audience – who had a better view of the black's route to the pocket than I did, because they were directly in line – began to cheer and shout, 'It's in'.

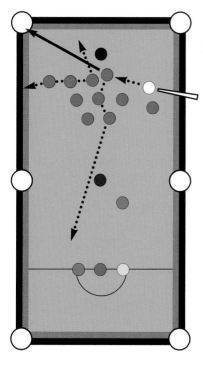

❶ Potting the red in question presented no real difficulty but the positional aspect of the shot was not so easy. In sinking the red I skimmed off the pack, left myself perfectly on the black and also took the opportunity to develop a couple of reds at the same time.

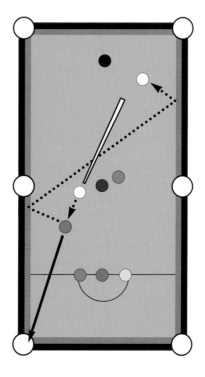

❷ Having knocked a single red towards baulk earlier in the break I always knew that a good shot would be required to both pot it and attain position on the black. I left the troublesome red until last, potted it to the green pocket and using stun and right hand side I managed to take the cue-ball off two cushions back to make the 15th black a straight-forward pot.

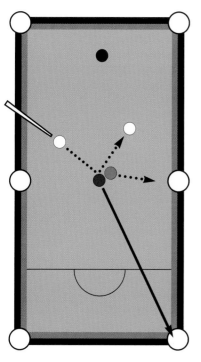

❸ John Spencer, a former world champion who was commentating on the match for the BBC, later called this the best shot he'd ever seen under pressure. In potting the blue, a tough assignment in itself, I also had to judge the cannon between cue-ball and pink. It was a great feeling when the blue found the heart of the baulk pocket and I chipped the pink nicely over the middle.

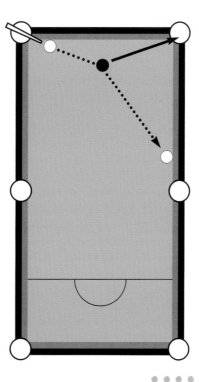

❹ Quite simply the biggest single shot of my career. Potting into a blind pocket is always tricky but I was determined, even under such intense pressure, to keep a clear head and cue it smoothly. As soon as the cue-ball and the black made contact I was pretty confident that I'd potted it and a split second later I suddenly became £163,000 richer.

GLOSSARY

ANGLED – A player is said to be angled if the path to the object-ball is obstructed or blocked by the jaws of a pocket.

BAULK – Baulk is the rectangular area of the table between the bottom cushion and the baulk line.

BREAK – This is a sequence of scoring shots. Numerically, a break is the number of points scored during this series of successful pots.

BREAK-OFF – The initial shot of every frame. A player places the cue-ball in the D and strikes it into the pyramid of reds. If the break-off is orthodox, the cue-ball deflects off the pack, off two cushions and returns to safety in baulk.

CHECK SIDE – Sidespin applied to the cue-ball which acts to narrow the angle at which it leaves the cushion. It also decreases the run of the cue-ball.

CLEARANCE – If a player comes to the table and pots all the balls remaining in a break, excepting the white, he is said to have fashioned a clearance. If the break includes fifteen reds, fifteen colours and the six colours in order, it is termed a total clearance.

CUE – A wooden piece of equipment, usually made of ash or maple, which is used by a player to strike the white.

CUE-BALL – The white ball struck by the cue in every shot.

CUE-BALL CONTROL – By using different spins, weight and angles, a player can position the white to his advantage. Positional play in a break means leaving your next pot easy. If you are playing safe, then cue-ball control helps a player to leave his opponent in as awkward a predicament as possible.

D – This is the surface area inside the semi-circle marked from the baulk line towards the bottom cushion.

DOUBLE – A pot which is completed after the object ball has come into contact with at least one cushion before entering the pocket.

DRAG – A positional device involving the application of backspin to allow the player to strike the cue-ball with authority but at a slow pace of approach to the object-ball.

EXTENSION – A relatively recent innovation, this is a tubular device attached to the cue and/or the ordinary rest to lengthen them and give a player much greater reach. Because of this, awkwardly placed shots, which used to require the cumbersome long rests, can now be played with your own cue and, therefore, tip.

FOUL STROKE – An illegal shot, for a variety of possible reasons, which leads to your opponent benefiting from the acquisition of penalty points, which themselves depend on the precise nature of the foul.

FRAME – This is the name given for one game. All competitive matches consist of a set number of frames. The name has its origins in the wooden or plastic triangular frame which is used to position the pyramid of reds at the start of the game.

FREE BALL – This is awarded to a player if, after a foul stroke by his opponent, he is snookered on the ball 'on'. In this instance a snooker is defined as a situation where both extreme edges of any object ball(s) cannot be hit. If a free ball is given, a player can nominate any of the six colours as a red. If it is successfully potted, he scores one point and goes on to select a colour as normal. If all of the reds have been potted, the free ball's value is equal to that of the lowest valued ball remaining on the table. After it has been potted the colours are then taken in their normal sequence. In the 1990 World Championship, Steve James took advantage of an early-frame free ball to fashion the first ever competitive sixteen red total clearance.

FULL BALL CONTACT – This arises when the cue-ball fully covers the object-ball at the precise moment of contact. It is the perfect contact for a dead straight pot.

IN HAND – If the cue-ball has been knocked off the table or, more commonly, it has gone in-off, it is said to be in hand. A player can then choose where to place the cue-ball in the D before restarting the frame.

IN-OFF – This occurs when the cue-ball accidentally goes into a pocket following contact with the object-ball. Penalty points arise from this, their value depending on the value of the ball 'on'.

JUMP SHOT – A foul stroke where, usually because of poor cue delivery, the cue-ball leaves the surface of the table and hops over the object-ball.

KICK – This is a general term applied to an abnormal contact between cue-ball and object-ball. It has a variety of causes, such as dirt on either ball, on the table or even static electricity in the atmosphere, but is virtually impossible to forecast. A kick can lead to either or both balls deviating violently from their normal path. Kicks can also dull the effects of topspin or screw by having a braking effect on the cue-ball.

KISS – An unintentional second contact on the object-ball by the cue-ball – known as a double kiss – or the cue-ball striking any other ball, either unintentionally or otherwise, after it has made initial contact with the object ball.

MAXIMUM BREAK – A player becomes a member of the exclusive maximum break club by potting fifteen reds, fifteen blacks (the highest value colour available) and then the six colours in sequence. With a free ball and an extra black, a 155 break – rather than the aforementioned

147 – is theoretically possible, although it has so far eluded even the very best of the game's exponents.

MISCUE – This is a stroke where, because of a lack of chalk on the tip, the awkward position of the cue-ball, or simply bad cueing, the contact between the tip of the cue and the cue-ball is not clean. This category of often expensive shots is more common when a player is attempting to impart side or backspin. A miscue sends the cue-ball off at an unpredictable angle and pace.

MISS – This has become one of the most discussed rules in snooker and often causes controversy. Basically, a miss is called when a referee does not believe a player has made a sufficiently good attempt to hit the ball 'on'. If a miss is called, there are three courses of action: the player of the miss can be asked to play again from the position in which the cue-ball has stopped; he can be asked to play again from the cue-ball's original position, which means that the referee has to replace the cue-ball; or the other player can take on the shot himself from where the cue-ball has come to rest. The rule, sensible in essence, was introduced as a means of preventing a player sacrificing a few penalty points in order to avoid leaving his opponent with a break-building opportunity. A competent referee takes into account the awkwardness of a shot as well as the overall standard of a player when deciding whether or not to call a miss. In professional snooker, since 1 January 1991, the rules have been much more rigid. If a player can see any part of the ball 'on' and fails to make contact, a miss is automatically called.

NAP – This is the grain of the cloth which runs from the baulk to the top end of a table. All shots can be affected by the nap, especially those played with sidespin or at a slow pace.

NATURAL ANGLE – The angle taken by the cue-ball after it has struck the object-ball. This assumes that the shot has been played at medium pace with no screw (backspin) or side imparted.

OBJECT-BALL – The ball needed to be hit first by the cue-ball.

PACK – The term used to describe the bunch of reds which are in a pyramid formation at the commencement of a frame.

PLANT – Any number of balls – two or more – can be involved in a plant. A successful plant occurs when the cue-ball makes contact with the object-ball in such a way that it knocks a second object-ball into a pocket.

POT – This is when the white strikes the object-ball, sending it into the pocket.

PUSH STROKE – A push stroke, not a legitimate shot in snooker, occurs when the tip of the cue, the cue-ball and object-ball come together simultaneously. Push strokes usually make a peculiar, distinctive sound and most often arise when cue-ball and object-ball are extremely close to each other.

REST – An accessory of the table the rest, which comes in various shapes and sizes, is an implement which allows a player to complete certain awkward shots that make a normal stance and bridge impossible to use.

RUNNING SIDE – Sidespin which widens the angle taken by the cue-ball after it has made contact with a cushion.

SAFETY STROKE – This is a tactical move, designed to leave your opponent in a position from which it is impossible, without an exceptional pot or a fluke, to initiate a scoring opportunity. The purpose of such a ploy is to try and force a mistake from your opponent.

SCREW – By striking the cue-ball below centre, screw – otherwise known as backspin – can be applied.

SET – This occurs when, with two balls touching in a certain way, the cue-ball can strike them in virtually any way to pot the second red.

SHOT TO NOTHING – An enviable position for a player, where he can attempt to pot the object-ball secure in the knowledge that, should he miss, the cue-ball will return to a safe position.

SIDE – A positional or safety aid, sidespin is applied to the cue-ball by striking it either to the left or right of centre.

SNOOKER – A player is snookered if his path to the object-ball is blocked by one or more intervening balls which make a direct path impossible. Escapes from a snooker involve either striking the cue-ball off at least one cushion or swerving the cue-ball.

SPIDER – A specially designed rest, which comes in several different forms, for bridging over intervening balls. It does this by providing a player with much greater elevation than a conventional rest.

STANCE – The posture a player adopts for his shots. It is a balanced stance which allows him to deliver the cue in a straight line through the cue-ball. Stances are not uniform, but all should have the common characteristic solidity.

STUN – A shot in which a degree of backspin is applied to the cue-ball, causing it to stop dead after making contact with the object ball. The amount of backspin required to achieve this effect, and therefore the point of contact on the cue-ball, depend on the pace of the shot and the distance between the cue-ball and the object-ball.

SWERVE – When an acute amount of sidespin is applied to the cue-ball, it leaves its normal path and curves. This shot, often called a masse, is used mostly by players trying to extract themselves from a snooker.

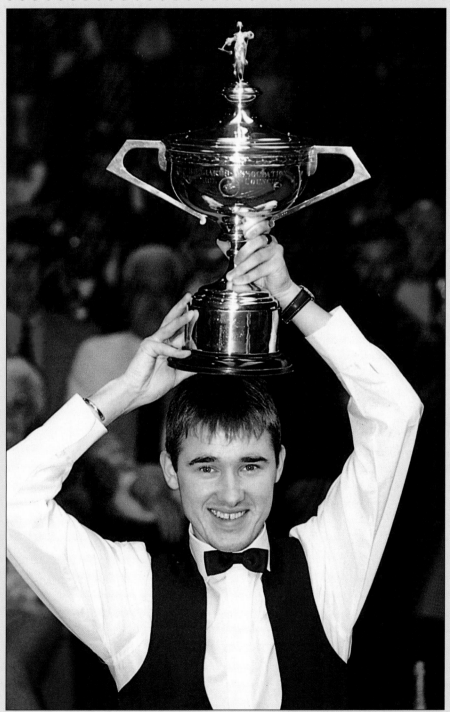

ERIC WHITEHEAD:
3, 7, 9, 10, 11, 13, 14, 15, 16, 17,
18, 19, 21, 22, 23, 25, 27, 28, 29,
30, 31, 32, 33, 34, 38, 40, 41, 42,
44, 45, 49, 50, 51, 52 (bottom), 53,
54, 55, 56, 57, 59, 60, 61, 74,
75, 78, 79, 104, 110, 127

ALLSPORT:
24 (Michael Cooper), 39 (Pascal Rondeau),
47, 52(top) (Howard Boylan),
81 (Michael Cooper), 95 (Howard Boylan),
96, 97 (Phil Cole), 98 (Michael Cooper), 99,
100 (Simon Bruty), 101 (Howard Boylan),
102 (Simon Bruty), 103 (Howard Boylan),
107 (Adrian Murrell), 109, 111,
112, 113 (Howard Boylan),114,
115, 117, 119, 120, 127 (Michael Cooper).